The
Banbury to Verney Junction
Branch

by
Bill Simpson

BUCKINGHAMSHIRE COUNTY LIBRARY

L.29

The
Banbury to Verney Junction Branch

by
Bill Simpson

Oxford Publishing Co

SBN 902888 87 0

ACKNOWLEDGEMENTS

The author wishes to proffer his heartfelt thanks to all of the following who have so generously and unstintingly supported his efforts to record this history.

All photographs are individually acknowledged.

Brian Garland, David Ratcliffe, Mr G.C.J. Hartland, J. Lowe, M. Morris, Mrs Whitney, Mr Cyril Gibbon, the late Arthur Elson, Arthur Grigg, Sid Sellers, Albert Woodward, Harry Tooth, 'Darby' Allan for the late Mrs Allan, Mrs Neville, Mr Earl, Roger Morgan, Mr H. Plant, Mr H. Somerton and Miss Somerton, A.N. Emerson, Dick Riley, Cheney & Sons (Printers) Banbury, Graham Wilton, Mr B. Trinder, Mr R.S. Hampson, Mrs K. Greenland, Christine Bloxham, T.J. Edgington (NRM), Mr N. Savings, Bert Williams, Harry Abbot, Blinkhorn's Photographers, Banbury, Mrs Waters, The Rev. B. Edmunds.

REFERENCES

Stratford-upon-Avon and Midland Junction Railway — the late J.M. Dunn.
The Railway Magazine 1910 and 1922.
Records of Buckinghamshire — 'Buckingham and the Railway' — R.S. Hampson.
'In Railway Service' — A.E. Grigg.
'A History of Banbury' — William Potts.
'History of the G.W.R.' — E.T. MacDermot, Ian Allan.
The Journal of Transport History, 'R.B. Dockray's Diary' — Michael Robbins (Leicester Univ. Press)
British Railway History vol. 1 — C. Hamilton Ellis. (George Allen & Unwin)
Banbury Guardian.
Buckingham Advertiser.
Brackley Advertiser.
'Drink and Sobriety' and 'An M.P. and his Constituents' — Barrie Trinder, B.A

Printed by Blackwell's in the City of Oxford

Published by
Oxford Publishing Co.,
8 The Roundway, Headington,
Oxford.

Foreword

Mr. Simpson has undertaken exhaustive and valuable research into the nostalgic and fascinating subject of the building of the Buckinghamshire Railway: because its life was so short and its landmarks are disappearing it is important that its history should be recorded before it is forgotten, and before its tradition of courtesy and resourcefulness is quite submerged beneath the inhumanity of the motorway and the selfishness of the motor car. Buckingham would be a more civilized place today if some of the heavy road vehicles which roar through its narrow streets could have their loads transferred back to the railway. Perhaps the container and the exhaustion of oil resources will one day herald a new railway age: its pioneers will find many guidelines in these pages.

I came across recently the menu card of the inaugural luncheon, held in the palm court of the newly completed Great Central Hotel at Marylebone station, of the last of our railways, the Great Central. My Grandfather was present, for he continued his father's welcome to the railways to build their tracks across his land. The menu was of eight courses, and on the back was a short note on the purpose of this great new railway "to provide a fast and reliable direct link between the industrial Midlands and the Channel Tunnel". That was in 1899. Perhaps when the Tunnel is eventually built that railway too will be needed again. Then there would again be two ways of getting from London to Buckingham by train, through Verney Junction.

Ralph Verney
25 July 1977

Introduction

Ever since steam locomotives appeared on railways in the early part of the 19th century they have engendered a strongly romantic appeal. To anyone who has witnessed this engineering phenomenon, whether in full cry or ambling along in some rather dilatory manner, the attraction is not surprising. To some extent this can also be regarded as a reflection of their early appearance, for even the numerous superlatives of the 20th century could hardly match the astonishment that must have been felt by the bystanders that could only stand and gape at the magical performance of an 'iron horse'.

In an age that has come to regard transportation and movement through the length and breadth of our isle as little more than commonplace, it is difficult for us in our well-heated, sleek, road machines to imagine that a twenty-mile journey was nothing short of an adventure to the mid-Victorians, hardly moving beyond the perimeter of town or village. Of course the early railways were not cheap, innovations of that magnitude seldom are and the poorer members were still only sightseers, but it gave credibility to their dreams and unquestionably altered their lives.

Being constructed in the very centre of the 19th century the Banbury line was such an innovation; I say line for in the early days of its construction it was more grandly acclaimed than a modest branch of the then Buckinghamshire Railway. But in the furore of early railway politics and speculation, that is in fact what it became, and for seventy years it served the community well in that role, if not very often the railway company's coffers.

In all of its 21¼ miles it was never more than a country line, serving small country towns and villages. The junction where it commenced its length, situated near Claydon, was no more than a hamlet surrounded by the green Buckinghamshire fields. To facilitate an introduction to its location I have decided to take a brief description along its length, separate from the finely detailed sections dealing with the individual stations.

Beginning at Banbury, where I sometimes think that the much rhymed "fine ladye on a whyte horse", would have been more appropriately seated upon a bullock, for the town has a long history as a farming and livestock trading centre. At Banbury the old Buckingham-shire station at the end of the branch is the closest point to the Great Western's Oxford — Birmingham line, only a few hundred yards separated their parallel positions. The approach to them both is situated in the valley of the Cherwell, which although pleasing is not exceptional by more worldly comparisons. Notwithstanding, any enthusiast of railways and locomotives would have found the location an absolute joy, as one could gaze down on the comings and goings of both railways, the shunting business and machinations of the steam loco-motive sheds without stirring from the valley heights. A world apart indeed.

After less than half a mile from the station the branch turned quite sharply away from its Western neighbour in an easterly direction.

A mile and a quarter from Banbury Warkworth crossing is reached, at this spot an old footpath between the local villages of Bodicote and Warkworth runs across the permanent way. The LNWR protected the safety of crossing the line by installing two large crossing gates with padlocks and built a tiny crossing-keepers house. Undoubtedly the most active period concerning the employee in this isolated dwelling would be after the construction of the Ministry of Munitions shell factory in the nearby fields, during the first world war. Today an elongated grassy mound bears evidence of the siding that ran from the crossing and into a fairly intensive railway system, serving the factory. With the passing of time all of this has disappeared. The crossing house was last occupied in the late 1950's and was demolished a few years later, as the ground returned to pasture, whilst the footpath continues to outlive the railway.

Beyond the crossing, continuing from Banbury, the first cutting is reached followed by two bridges in close proximity. The first runs beneath the railway to Overthorpe from Kings Sutton, the second strides a single arch above the line and leads to Middleton Cheney. The line is now climbing to the summit of Cockley Brake. Before the summit is reached however there was the intermediate station of Farthinghoe (MP 18). The country station has been eulogised throughout its age not only by lovers of railways but by writers and artists alike; it is as if its pastoral timelessness recalled some almost forgotten prospect of tranquillity. In this respect Farthinghoe was most surely an archetype. After Farthinghoe there is a large stone viaduct crossing the A422 Brackley to Banbury road. One of its five arches also strides a long avenue of trees that leads in a very picturesque fashion from the A422 road to the village of Thenford, in later years it became known by the locals and the railway staff as the 'Avenue Bridge'. Continuing the climb to Cockley Brake Junction (MP 16), where the line from Towcester and

Helmdon joined the branch, one soon passed beyond the open vista of cows and sheep grazing in spacious fields and entered a fairly deep cutting. Nearby in the shuttered gloom of Cockley Wood the echoing shrill cries of the birds would be disturbed by the roar of a climbing locomotive. The junction is once again more openly situated and the line then commences a curve to the south, skirting a hill, thus avoiding the need for a tunnel. Many footpaths were crossed by the line and midway between Cockley Brake and Brackley one footpath meanders down a hill to end at the lineside. This footpath runs from the nearby Manor House of Stean Park and in the early days of the railway's survey it was agreed as part of a condition for allowing the railway access onto his lands, that the lord of the manor would have facility of a request stop. This was called Stean Park Halt (MP 14½) although the only furnishings appear to be a gate from the field. Memories of its usage are scant and no engineman ever recalls being requested to stop there. Between Stean Park Halt and Brackley was the most aptly named Skew Bridge, this carried the A422 road above the railway. A glance at the map and photographs will show how very severe the skew angle was to the rails, almost parallel. It was constructed with space to accept two running lines but in the event only one was ever used, whether or not the structure was a design of inherent weakness I do not know, one thing is certain and this is that the unused space beside the running line was occupied with some very heavy buttressing in later years. After the section of road carried by the bridge had been replaced by a short by-pass in 1976 the bridge was partly demolished.

Beyond Brackley (MP 12) to Buckingham the river Ouse threads the course of the railway with several intersections of the line. The countryside is very rustic, farms and small villages retain to this day a sleepy detachment from any kind of change and but for the removal of lines and new tarmacadam road, the crossing at Bacon's House appears to have altered little since before the railway's arrival.

A mile and a half beyond Brackley station is the sight of the still remaining Great Central Railway bridge crossing above the branch at a skew angle. Built with the arrival of that railway in 1892, with the new main line from London to the Midlands and a competing station for the old company at Brackley. Just over a mile and two miles further is the station and crossings of Fulwell and Westbury (MP 9) and Bacon's House (MP 7¾).

Water Stratford and Radclive are two villages near Buckingham that received a belated service from the railway in the last decade of its existence. Radclive crossing has another small railway house that had an attendant keeper for supervising the gates of the footpath from the village.

The next railway installation is beneath the bridge that carries the Tingewick Road into Buckingham, this is the Buckingham station goods yard. To this day the rotting timber goods shed is standing with its simple 'gallows' crane with a single pulley wheel on a central swivel fixed to the goods platform. Remaining also is a brick-built stable which now garages a local coal merchants lorry, for the purpose of which the land continues to be used — storing coal.

After the substantial town of Buckingham there are only 4½ miles left to Verney Junction; halfway was the tiny station of Padbury with its low cobble platform and single station building that are now obliterated beneath a new housing estate. There was a second skew bridge after Padbury, this time the railway crossed the village road just outside the station, the skew on this bridge was by no means as severe as the one mentioned north of Brackley. Close by the line at Padbury is the mound of Norbury, a relic of a much older iron age where it is believed that a raised enclosure of some fifteen acres once held a smallholding and cattle. A few miles further and the branch closes with the Oxford and Bletchley double track branch at Verney Junction. A capacious installation considering its isolation and I daresay a welcome refuge if one were wintering amidst those open Buckinghamshire fields whilst changing trains.

That then is by way of a brief introduction to the course of the Banbury branch, a permanent way from 1850 until 1968. The details of its life story are contained within the text and is belaboured no further by epitaphs from me. Being one of a large breed of a widespread system many of its vagaries will be familiar, at the same time — like the pattern of the snowflake — no two are exactly the same. My earnest wish is that I may have helped to highlight some of the jewels of its individuality.

Bill Simpson

Banbury, Oxfordshire.

Crown Copyright, National Railway Museum, York.

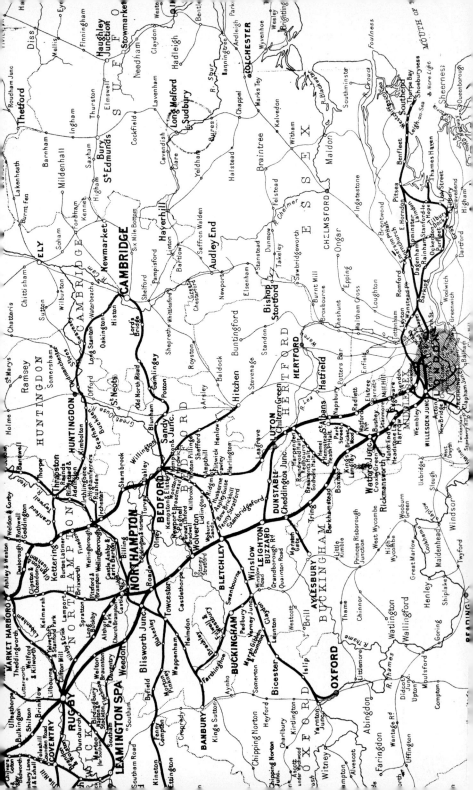

Chapter One

The Historical Background

When the London and Birmingham Railway was opened on 17th September, 1838 it passed through the county of Buckinghamshire but it did not serve it with any station. Hitherto the county had had the substantial support of the Grand Union Canal, with a branch to Aylesbury, the county town, and another to Buckingham. The Aylesbury townspeople were by no means dilatory in seeing the opportunities that a new railway could offer and wasted little time in forming a company under Robert Stephenson to build a branch from the L&B at Cheddington; this was duly opened in June, 1839.

At this time Aylesbury had a highly perceptive and energetic Member of Parliament, a Baronet and local land owner by the name of Sir Harry Verney. Sir Harry was aware of the L&B's interest in some lines passing through the county and together with His Grace the second Duke of Buckingham (Grenville-Temple) they pooled their ideas for bringing an extensive railway service to the people and development of the basic agricultural interests therein.

Together with the support of the L&B two separate companies were formed, the Buckingham and Brackley Junction Railway and the Oxford and Bletchley Junction Railway. Later under the direction of the newly formed London & North Western Railway the two were merged into a unified board with the collective name of the Buckinghamshire Railway, in 1847. With the formation of the two companies the chairmanship was occupied by the Duke of Buckingham. However, following some financial difficulties at Stowe, the Duke's home near Buckingham, he was forced to retire from the board. The family interest did not cease as his son the Marquess of Chandos took a seat on the board, but the chairmanship was succeeded by Sir Harry.

As I shall subsequently describe, the layout of the lines existed as a relic of the unfulfilled objectives of the L&B and LNWR. In their final form they ran westward from Bletchley to Oxford, via Winslow and Bicester, with a junction near Claydon House (later Verney Junction) the home of Sir Harry Verney where another line turned north to Brackley via Buckingham, with a further extension to Banbury (9 miles 5 furlongs and 2¾ chains). The first survey with the L&B included a southern arm leaving from the same junction and reaching as far to the metropolis as Harrow. However high costs and the railway politics of the day caused this plan to be abandoned although it was to be adopted in later proposals as an extension to Aylesbury. As a result three bills were

e layout of lines in the Buckinghamshire and Oxfordshire area before 1890.

9

placed before Parliament, two for the previously independent companies in 1846. The third, in 1847, was to effect the establishment of the newly amalgamated companies into the Buckinghamshire Railway and to be granted extension of lines from Brackley to Banbury and from Claydon to Aylesbury. During 1847 plans to construct the southern arm across the Vale of Aylesbury, were petitioned against by the LNWR and probably grieved Sir Harry Verney who seemed very keen to see the system applied in its entirety, viz:

Aylesbury to Harrow	33 miles
Aylesbury to Tring	9 miles
Verney Junction to Aylesbury	12 miles
Verney Junction to Oxford	21 miles
Bletchley to Banbury	31 miles
TOTAL	106 miles

The engineer employed to build the Buckinghamshire Railway was no less a person than Robert Stephenson with a labour force contracted through the offices of Thomas Brassey.

In the preceding account I have endeavoured to describe the Buckinghamshire Railway in purely local terms, which indeed it never was. The original concept of a railway crossing the Vale of Aylesbury to Birmingham was promulgated as early as 1825 by George and Robert Stephenson of the then London and Birmingham Railway. A survey carried out by them had envisaged the main line running from Tring, to Aylesbury, Buckingham, Banbury and Birmingham. Because of objections raised by the 1st Duke of Buckingham and the amount of political pressure that he was able to apply, the railway had to be re-routed away from the Duke's lands and take a course through Leighton Buzzard, Wolverton and Castlethorpe.

Up to the year 1844 Buckinghamshire had been poorly served by railways with only the Aylesbury connection to the L&B in the east, whilst the Great Western's new Oxford Line was well beyond the county boundaries to the west. This left the area as a no-man's-land and bait for a railway hungry age.

It would I feel overburden the local branch line atmosphere intended by this history to follow every political twist and turn in the widespread confusion of the "Railway Mania", but keeping as close to the fundamental issues as possible one must nevertheless try to describe broadly and concisely each subsequent step that affected the fortune and demise of this eventful line.

The first shot came from the Great Western in 1844 who placed before Parliament two bills for schemes north of Oxford, the first for a company called the Oxford, Worcester and Wolverhampton Railway and the second for the Oxford and Rugby Railway. The fact that the Great Western was continuing to push two broad gauge schemes north of Oxford, in the teeth of opposition from the Gauge Commission (who implemented the Gauge Act of 1846 and opposed the extension of the wider gauge beyond that city), reveals some interesting political juggling amongst the notables of the day.

A certain Captain Mark Huish, Secretary of the Grand Junction Railway in the north was highly desirous of amalgamating the London and Birmingham company with his own, from which the latter would derive every benefit. So at the very same time that the balance was tilting slightly against the broad gauge he weighed in heavily in its favour, singing its praises beyond Birmingham to the north and supporting a Birmingham and Oxford Junction company intended to connect with the proposed Oxford and Rugby at Fenny Compton. As he did so he castigated the London and Birmingham for its plans to create a virtual monopoly in all the territories south of Birmingham. Part of these plans was the London and Birmingham's opposing bill, allied with the Midland Railway, to form the London, Worcester and South Staffordshire Railway, including the two former companies of the Buckinghamshire Railway. The route of this line followed similarly to that of George Stephenson's survey some eighteen years earlier, leaving the main line at Tring and running through Aylesbury, Bicester, Banbury turning west at Fenny Compton to Evesham, Worcester and Wolverhampton. Part of the scheme included branches from Bicester to Oxford and from Banbury to Rugby, thus being a complete attempt to counter the two broad gauge schemes of the Great Western.

In the light of these events to say that the people of towns like Banbury were confused is something of an understatement.

In 1844 H.W. Tancred, MP for Banbury entered enthusiastically into the efforts of his Banbury friends to bring a railway to the town, being willing, on this issue, to comply with whatever were the wishes of his constituents. It seems that in the battle with the broad and narrow gauge schemes, Tancred identified himself closely with the narrow gauge Buckinghamshire railways with which Cobb's Bank was associated. He passed on to one of his correspondents the optimistic prophesies of Samuel Carter, solicitor to the London & Birmingham Railway and arranged meetings at his club between Carter and Cobb to discuss railway matters.

During the confusion of 1844 the two companies continued to look for support in the Borough. A meeting in Banbury early in July supported the GWR scheme, whilst a petition recorded in May had favoured a narrow gauge Oxford — Rugby route.

The companies struck their colours and battle was joined in the parliamentary session of 1845, the Great Western safe in the knowledge that their powerful ally Mark Huish and the Birmingham and Oxford Railway would make a case for running (in theory at any rate) far north and into the lines of the Grand Junction itself, at the same time claiming access to London, independent of the L&B. Both bills passed through the Commons and into committee stage along with several other rival narrow gauge schemes.

The debate lasted for a month with over a hundred witnesses being called, many of them being industrialists from the affected areas. Amongst the railway engineers there were several famous names including Robert Stephenson and R.B. Dockray of the L&B (of the latter we shall hear more concerning the Banbury branch), also William Cubitt, Brunel and the notorious Captain Huish.

The final result was a defeat for the L&B and its allies who were forced to withdraw, thus continuing the advancement of broad gauge beyond Oxford, tempered by the addition of a single clause obliging the Great Western to lay in a third rail to allow for the use of narrow gauge traffic, this being done by inserting a rail inside the broad gauge. This defeat left the two constituent companies that formed the Buckinghamshire Railway falling well short of the greater aims of the L&B and also forcing that company into an amalgamation with the Grand Junction.

No sooner was the ink dry on the documents that proclaimed the London and North Western Railway than Huish withdrew his company's support for the Birmingham and Oxford who naturally looked to the GWR for support, but remaining still as an individual company. It is interesting to note that nowhere had they been pressed in the matter of gauge.

The details of the tug-of-war between the GWR and the newly formed LNWR to capture the O&B are perfectly described in Macdermot's 'History of the GWR' suffice to say that it was very involved with further examples of the nefarious schemes of Captain Huish's financial baiting and political cajolement ending finally with the Birmingham and Oxford being ceded to the GWR in 1848.

During this period the graphic situation in Buckinghamshire, Northamptonshire and Oxfordshire was one of delay for the Oxford and Rugby until the replacement of a tardy contractor, but they were now building with all speed to Fenny Compton, whilst the Buckinghamshire Railway on the other side were making all speed towards Banbury, every bridge and abutment being built to allow double track. At what point the LNWR realised that the Birmingham & Oxford was lost to them it is impossible to ascertain. The Gauge Commissioners although sympathising with what appeared to be a lost cause for the Buckinghamshire line of the LNWR seemed nervous about allowing the broad gauge only to continue on the Birmingham and Oxford with some foreboding on the issue of mixed gauge. This led to another conflagration between the 'old enemies' of the LNWR and GWR resulting in a mixed gauge being decreed for the line throughout, upon which the LNWR acquired running powers with all 'proper and convenient accommodation in respect of stations, sidings, waiting and watering places and various other facilities', also, 'for engines and carriages to and from the several narrow-gauge railways which do or shall communicate therewith respectively.' The document further contains a clause insisted upon by the LNWR — that the GWR should not be entitled to use the broad gauge rails until a narrow gauge connection has been made with the former in the city of Birmingham. And with these clauses the bill received the Royal Assent in August, 1848, by which time the line to Banbury was very well advanced. Curiously the running powers existing in these clauses were never exercised, nor according to Robert Stephenson were they ever intended to be, the responsibility for them being with the LNWR's solicitor Carter, who had secured them out of spite and partly to appease the Bucks Railway.

In 1849 the two rival companies must have been working almost "cheek by jowl" with each other in the town of Banbury and must have provided the borough with some interesting moments, especially on pay nights.

It was decided by the GWR to open their route as single line with "one engine in steam" working and as there was no prospect of a connection with any other line, to leave it as broad gauge for the time being. They also abandoned their original plan for the line to Rugby from Fenny Compton. To this effect they wrote to the Railway Commissioners applying to postpone the instalment of the third rail. The Commissioners sent a copy of this letter to the Buckinghamshire Railway of the LNWR whose chief Mark Huish was much aggrieved and despatched Edward Watkin, Secretary of the Bucks Railway to attend to this matter. Watkin upbraided the Commissioners upon their business, that they had already sanctioned the line to open only when the 4'8½'' 'national' gauge had been installed along its full length, and as the matter was now mandatory could see no further reason for discussion. He stated further that it was the intention of the directors of the Bucks Railway to apply to the GWR for a narrow gauge connection at Banbury.

It has been well chronicled elsewhere that this connection could not possibly be of any value to the LNWR and this was probably the case. On the other hand I am quite sure that the Buckinghamshire Railway was keen to see a connection had the climate been less stormy between the warring companies. Indeed a connection was installed some thirteen years later when the third rail was in situ on the broad gauge. As described in the minutes of a board meeting of the Buckinghamshire Directors dated in 1863, that such a connection had been agreed and installed for 'the facility of an interchange of traffic'. It was therefore no surprise that Sir Harry Verney's voice should be heard above the clamour upon this very issue. Captain Simmons reported back to the Commissioners regarding the fact that as no narrow gauge completion was imminent he could not see how the interests of the public could be injuriously affected by opening the line in broad gauge only, provided that the GWR undertook to lay the third rail when the line was extended northwards. Upon this issue there followed another round of quarrelling between the two larger companies and their leaders, Huish and Watkin versus Saunders, secretary of the GWR and the vicarious Railway Commissioners, and as I previously mentioned including the voice of the Buckinghamshire, Sir Harry Verney. The conclusion of all this was that the GWR were strictured to fulfil their agreement within four months, or face legal action by the Commissioners; in fact, two

Sir Harry Verney by George Richmond. A portrait that hangs in the Monument
Room at Claydon House, circa 1860.

Sir Ralph Verney

more years were to pass before they did so. Needless to say the Commissioners did not embark upon a lengthy and expensive legal suit on so minor an issue.

The GWR line was opened between Oxford and Banbury on Monday, 2nd September, 1850 four months after the Banbury branch. In July 1851 the Buckinghamshire Railway, which by original Acts had reached agreement first with the London and Birmingham and then with subsequent London and North Western, to hire all locomotives and rolling stock from the parent company, leased the lines to the LNWR for 999 years.

Even though the LNWR had lost the day in Banbury, they would by now be able to sense some rumblings of dissent from within the Western empire; this was coming from the board room of that offspring of the GWR the Oxford, Worcester and Wolverhampton Railway. Accounts of the final eruption are amply chronicled elsewhere; insomuch as it affects the Buckinghamshire Railway, this brought about an agreement between the OWW and the LNWR for the latter to construct a narrow gauge connection north of Oxford at Yarnton providing the larger Company with its subsequent and valedictory access to the West Midlands that had been lost by the London and Birmingham at Banbury. For the OWW it was to be their first narrow gauge outlet to the south, opened in 1854. This agreement lasted some twenty one years but was only lucrative to the Buckinghamshire Railway up to 1856, when the offspring returned to the Western fold under its new name, the West Midland's Railway.

It is interesting to note that each half-yearly report showed the Buckinghamshire to be gaining a moderate prosperity and a fair return; when however the valuable freight was re-routed through Oxford and Didcot, together with a nationwide depression in railway shares, the Buckinghamshire sank into the red, from which it never re-emerged.

On the matter of financial returns Sir Harry Verney had taken issue with Euston from the outset, arguing that had the lines originally envisaged been completed they should have provided a lucrative exchange, from Harrow in the south to Wolverhampton in the north and by connections through Oxford to Bristol in the west and similarly to Norwich in the east. He complained that all manner of goods from Buckingham to Birmingham must still go via Bletchley as there was still no connection with the Birmingham and Oxford. The line from Claydon to Aylesbury was a particularly thorny issue upon which the LNWR had stood adamant. In Sir Harry's view this line was the artery of the system and a much needed link with the county town, whilst the LNWR continued to point out that they already served Aylesbury via Cheddington, a line which Sir Harry had been active in creating. After a great deal of energy had been expended and at no little financial cost to himself, Sir Harry did see this line built by the LNWR who remained coldly hostile to the construction of Verney Junction and exchange sidings.

Nevertheless the Buckinghamshire soldiered on until Saturday, 23rd February, 1878 when Richard Moon, Chairman of the LNWR was elected onto the Board; by 15th July, in the same year the consolidation of the Company's shares with those of the LNWR had taken place, and the Buckinghamshire Railway was no more.

As for the Banbury branch, there was now an exchange siding and a gasworks siding connecting the old enemies together at Banbury. The war was over at last and with the territory north and west of Banbury firmly in Great Western hands it seemed unlikely that Banbury LNWR would ever develop beyond a 'temporary' terminal station.

252.—NORTHAMPTON AND BANBURY JUNCTION.

Incorporated by 26 and 27 Vic., cap. 220 (28th July, 1863), to construct a line from Blisworth, on the London and North Western, to the Banbury Extension of the Buckinghamshire. Length, 18 miles. Capital, 140,000*l.* in 10*l.* shares, and 46,000*l.* on loan. Extra land, two acres; compulsory purchase. three years; completion of works, five years. Arrangements with London and North Western.

No. of Directors — 5; minimum, 4; quorum, 3. *Qualification*, 300*l.*

DIRECTORS:

Alexander Beattie, Esq.
Cooke Baines, Esq.
William Gregory, Esq.

Robert Stanton Wise, Esq.
George James Eady, Esq.

Notice of the Company of the Northampton and Banbury Junction Railway in Bradshaw's Shareholder's Guide 1864.

Rev. B. Edmunds

7.—BILLS LODGED FOR SESSION 1864.

The subjoined list comprises a detail of the whole of the Bills lodged, in compliance with the standing orders of both Houses of Parliament, in the Private Bill Office, o 23rd December last :—

Blockley and Banbury.—Incorporation of company; construction of railway from the Great Western, at Blockley, to the Buckinghamshire at Banbury; working agreements with the London and North Western and Great Western; amendment of acts.

Blyth and Tyne.—Additional powers; purchase of wayleaves and lands; additional share and loan capital; preference shares; amendment of acts, &c.

Bills lodged for Session 1864 Blockley and Banbury.

Rev. B. Edmunds

16

Chapter Two

The Opening of the Banbury Branch

At 5 pm on Tuesday, 20th April, 1847 near the Cross Keys public house in the Landborough Road, Buckingham, the first sod of the Buckinghamshire Railway was turned by a Mr Field, a Physician of the firm of Thomas Brassey. Amongst those present was the appointed local agent a Mr Horn, with offices in Castle Street. The little ceremony passed almost totally unnoticed and was not attended by any of the leading figures of the day.

The slumbering Buckingham was soon awakened when the large numbers of navvies that prelude the building of a railway descended thereon. The Corporation complained, as Corporations must, of several violations, one concerning the water cart that continually blocked the Tingewick Road bridge, whilst the police were forced to provide maximum strength for Saturday night patrols. Overnight the town turned into a hard drinking and riotous centre, so difficult to imagine when one walks through its charming little streets today. Not surprisingly the Board of Directors felt morally obliged to take some action to quell this state of affairs that they had brought upon the peaceful countryside. A minute of the Board dated in 1847 read thus, "The Directors have taken measures for promoting the moral and religious instruction of the workmen employed upon the line, and of their children. In this object they have liberally seconded Mr Brassey the contractor for the work". In effect what this meant was that the company employed a full time Chaplain and a number of scripture readers, and always expected the traditions of the Sabbath to be observed, even though the same individuals had been reduced to brawling intemperance the night before.

In the sober world of finance the line was meeting some heavy commitments and in a period of economic restraint railway capital was becoming more frugal. A letter addressed to the Board of Directors from their Secretary Edward Watkin, early in 1849, says that the cash flow had reduced somewhat and that economies were advisable in order to keep progress toward the planned opening of the system early in the next decade. "The line to Banbury is so advanced as to be near complete, some saving may be made if it remained as a single line until, and as when traffic would warrant a second line of rails to be laid". He continued; "The line between Claydon and Oxford is temporarily suspended at Islip in order to pursue work on the more financially remunerative line to Banbury."

Here is therefore a brief statement of the financial situation that hung over the venture:

BUILDING COSTS

	£
Total building cost for all lines from Bletchley to Banbury and from Claydon Junction to Islip	1,078,389
1847 — 1849 Brackley to Bletchley	339,612
1847 — 1849 Brackley to Banbury	100,988

Division of Amounts paid 1849 — Bletchley to Banbury.

Land for line and stations	151,000
Rails and Chairs	99,000
Works	288,000

Expenditure required to complete a double line from Bletchley to Banbury

Land, line and stations	9,000
Cost of Works	187,817

Of rails and chairs, sufficient had already been purchased.

COST OF STATIONS

Stations	Amount	Turntables and Other Machinery
	£	£
*Padbury	2,500	500
Buckingham	4,870	1,000
*Finmere	1,160	300
Brackley	3,994	1,050
Farthinghoe	3,115	500
Banbury	7,000	2,000

* Even though these stations are costed here it would seem that they fell victim of economies as no such stations were opened between Buckingham and Brackley until Fullwell & Westbury in 1879, whilst Padbury was not opened until 1878.

The authorised share capital of the Oxford and Bletchley Junction Railway was £500,095 with powers to borrow a further £198,000. The capital of the Buckingham and Brackley Junction Railway was £200,000 with borrowing powers for a further £66,666, the Banbury extension being paid for by the LNWR.

1 mentioned earlier in the section dealing with the political history of the branch a certain Mr R.B. Dockray; you will remember that he assisted the unsuccessful attempt by the London and Birmingham to counter the Great Western's Oxford, Worcester and Wolverhampton line.

Robert Benson Dockray (1811-1871) had established himself high amongst the respected railway engineers of the day; well experienced with difficulties, he was integrally involved in the construction of the London to Birmingham line. In 1840 he became engineer-in-charge of the Banbury branch, amongst others, and was therefore familiar with those early days of construction; thankfully he also kept a diary of events, which reveals a fascinating personal account of situations that occurred 125 years ago.

26th March, 1850. . . "This morning a large party consisting of Mr Brassey and his assistants, some of the directors, the engineers and the traffic managers of the Buckinghamshire Railway went to Bletchley and passed from thence to Banbury per special train, stopping to examine the stations, which were much approved for their businessslike look and absence of all unnecessary ornament. . . We returned to Winslow where at 3 o'clock we sat down to a very handsome dinner served in the goods shed. The whole area was boarded over level with the platform and lined throughout like a tent with red and white bunting. There were a 120 persons and the dinner was served quite hot, temporary kitchens had been built adjoining. I had to propose Mr Brassey's health. . . The works on the line evidently made a good impression — in fact it only wants traffic to be quite a pet."

19th April, 1850. . . "This morning Captn. Wynne, Inspector of Railways, examined the Buckinghamshire Railway from Bletchley to Banbury. We had a special train and left Euston immediately after the 9 o'clock train, taking up Captn. Wynne at Harrow station where he resides for the purpose of educating his boys. It appears that the Railway Commission has not finally passed the Rugby and Stamford nor will do so until completed. I have no doubt they will act just the same on the Buckinghamshire — indeed one cannot see the object of these inspections by an officer of the Government unless it be to ascertain that all necessary (for) the convenience and safety of the traffic are ready.

At Bletchley we met the remainder of our party, and formed the train consisting of two engines and tenders which we took in order to test the iron bridges and two carriages. We had with us in addition to our engineering staff Messrs. Watkin, Bruyeres, McConnel, Mills and Norris — Mr Horne was also with us.

The day was unfavourable, it rained nearly all the time. Captn. Wynne, Dixon and myself rode on the first engine, we stopped at all the under bridges and examined them. At the wrought iron girder at Padbury we ran the train backwards and forwards, taking the deflection with a level — it was found to be .02 of a foot for the centre girder and .04 the outside, which Captn. W. pronounced very satisfactory. Some of the bridges near Beacon's Wood are much shattered by the frost, the stone splitting and the spandrels bulged. I ordered one in particular to be rebuilt with all possible despatch. At the great bridge for the Banbury

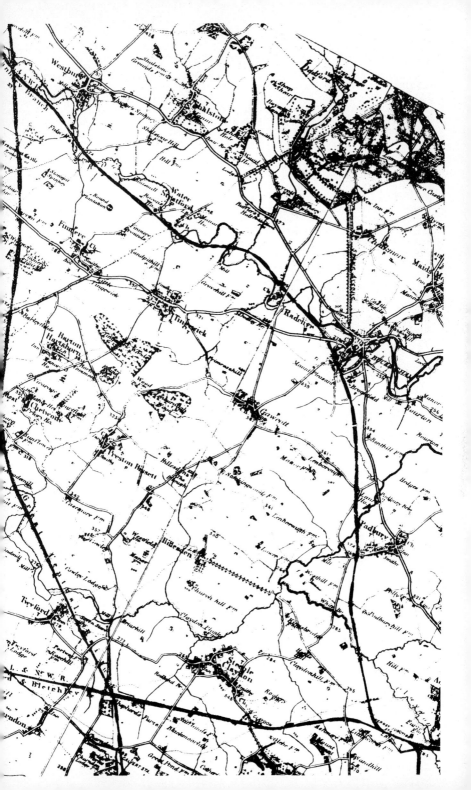

53.—BUCKINGHAMSHIRE.

An amalgamation of the BUCKINGHAM AND BRACKLEY, incorporated by 10 Vic , cap. 233 (1846), and of the OXFORD AND BLETCHLEY, incorporated 10 Vic., cap. 82 (1846), under the present title, by 10 and 11 Vic., cap 236 (1847), with further powers for an extension of the former scheme north to Banbury, and South to Aylesbury—10 miles ; Bletchley to Oxford, 31½ miles, with a line from Claydon to a junction with the Great Western, Oxford and Rugby, at Banbury—21½ miles. Total, 53 miles. Of this there is 21 miles 34 chains single line, and 31 miles 5 chains with double rails. The amount authorised by the Extension Act of 1847 (450,000*l.*) was provided by the London and North Western. An act was obtained in 1853, to authorise a junction with the Oxford, Worcester, and Wolverhampton, near Oxford. The whole undertaking is leased from 1st July, 1851, for 999 years, under act 11 and 12 Vic., cap. 236, to the London and North Western, at 4 per cent. per annum, with half surplus profits ; as, however, the whole of the extension capital is found by the lessees, their actual liability is limited to payment of dividend on the *original* 17½*l.* shares=195,000*l.*

It was reported in August that the aggregate receipts during the half-year showed an increase both in passengers and merchandise as compared with the corresponding period of 1862. The local receipts also contrasted favourably, and there had been a considerable amount of traffic with the district lately opened out by means of the new line from Bedford to Cambridge. The London and North Western Company are about, by means of new junctions, to connect the lines of this company at Banbury and Oxford with those of the Great Western, for the purpose of facilitating the interchange cf traffic at those places.

The meetings are held in London, in February and August, for declaration of dividend, due 30th June and 31st December. Certificates must accompany transfer stock Registration fee 2*s.* 6*d.* each deed. The company will transfer 10*s.* of stock.
Scale of Voting.—C. C. C. Act, sec. 75.
No. of Directors.—Maximum, 18 ; minimum, 9. *Qualification*, 50 shares=875*l.* stock.

DIRECTORS.

Chairman—Sir HARRY VERNEY, Bart , M.P., South Street, Park Lane, W., and Claydon House, Buckinghamshire.

Robert Benson, Esq., Craven Hill Gardens, Hyde Park, W.	Matthew Lyon, Esq., Leamington.
Timothy Rhodes Cobb, Esq., Banbury.	Major E. Dewes, Buckingham.
Richard Ryder Dean, Esq., Gloucester Place, Portman Square, W.	The Right Hon. the Earl of Camperdown Hill Street, Berkeley Square, W.
The Hon. Arthur Kinnaird, M.P., Pall Mall East, S.W.	G. C Glyn, Esq., M.P., Lombard Street E.C.
His Grace the Duke of Buckingham, Stowe, Buckinghamshire.	The Hon. Philip Sydney Pierrepont, Eveney Hall, Brackley.
	Thomas Young, Esq., Eaton Square, S.W

The Directors retire from office in rotation, in the alphabetical order of their names. All eligible for re-election.

OFFICERS.—Sec., William Long ; Auditors, Capt. Thomas Porter, R.N., and Richard Carter, Buckingham.

Offices—Euston Station, London, N.W.

List of directors and details of the Buckinghamshire Railway Company as they appeared in Bradshaw's Shareholders Guide, 1864. Note the line referring to the much hoped for connection by the Buckinghamshire with the G.W.R. at Banbury — thus the northern access.

Rev. B. Edmonds

turnpike road we stopped a long time, its magnitudes and construction surprised Capt. W much. . . Capt. W. noted that we had deviated our levels beyond the limit's and had made one level crossing where we ought by the Act to have placed a bridge. On the whole I am pleased with Capt. Wynne, he is a quiet gentlemanlike man.''

Buckinghamshire Railway.

SEVENTEENTH HALF-YEARLY GUARANTEED DIVIDEND,

At 4 per Cent. per Annum, to 31st Dec., 1859.

		£	s.	d.
Half-Year's Dividend on £ 140	Stock at 4 per Cent. per Annum...	2	16	—
	Less Income Tax, 9d. in the Pound............	—	2	1
	(Being 3 Months at 1s. and 3 Months at 5d.)			
	£	2	13	11

OFFICE, EUSTON STATION, LONDON, N.W.,
28th *February*, 1860.

SIR,

I am instructed to send you the above Statement, and the Draft
annexed for the Dividend due.

I am desired also to request your *particular* attention to the Notes at the foot of the
Warrant, and to beg that you will not fail to give timely notice of any change in your
residence, that the Warrants for your future Dividends may not be mis-sent.

I am, SIR,

Your obedient Servant,

WILLIAM LONG,
Secretary.

☞ This **HALF SHEET** to be retained, the **OTHER** to be presented to the
Bankers entire.

Buckinghamshire Railway statement of seventeenth half-yearly dividend.

Norman A. Savings

On April 23rd permission to open was withheld until completion of
the sidings.

29th April 1850. . . "This morning I went to the Buckinghamshire
Railway with Capt. Laffan, the Government Inspector, to view the
works preparatory to the opening next Wednesday. Capt. Wynne had
made an inspection on the 19th but would not pass the line until the
points and crossings and other works principally at the Banbury
station were in a more forward state. A large party joined us, the
principal officers of the Company and several of the Buckinghamshire
Directors, Capt. Laffan is a gentlemanlike young man, of good presence
and I should think well qualified for his place. He said that he merely
wished to see the works to which Capt. Wynne had objected. He rode
on the engine, stopping at the stations and examining the points and
crossings. He made some good suggestions about not laying down
points until the sidings were ready to receive them, otherwise the
engine might take the points and run off the road."

1st May 1850. . . "This morning the Buckinghamshire Railway was opened for the passenger traffic from Bletchley to Banbury. There are four trains each way per day. It will make quite a social revolution in the district which until the opening of this line may said to have been almost cut off from the (?outside, entire) world. The opening of the railway in the eastern, western, and central parts (of England) having diverted from it all the old stage coaches which used formerly to afford the means of communication; so that unless by the expensive means of posting it was no easy matter to move about among the little towns of Buckinghamshire."

On this observation it would appear that the stagecoaches disappeared well before the railway opened, thus returning the community to an isolation hardly experienced in its living memory. Fortunately the new railway was able to restore this serious void in communication almost immediately. It is noted that 7,072 passengers were carried along its metals in excursion trains to the Great Exhibition of 1851, in the period from 5th May to 3rd August.

15th May, 1850. . . "I went to Banbury. The coals and goods traffic opens today. Things are in a very unfinished state especially at Buckingham; however, they can manage to make a beginning. The works have everywhere been pushed with remarkable energy and I am only surprised that they are not more behind. Last night the coal owners in their eagerness to outstrip each other actually sent 100 wagons, sufficient I should imagine to stock the line for three months at this season of the year. It inconvenienced us very much. John Dockray was up all night making arrangements for their reception."

It is difficult to imagine in an age that is so familiar with mechanical transportation, of the exhilarating effect upon the townspeople of the mid-nineteenth century created by the opening of the railway. This was the first line to arrive at Banbury, something that Banburians had hitherto only heard of briefly in handbills, posters or by word of mouth. Unreachable London was coming within the grasp of many who knew it only as a legendary place, cattle and goods could be despatched to arrive at faraway Southampton, at least within two days! Against the background of this imaginative age with its adventure in steam the excited townspeople were not going to let opening of the line pass without due celebration.

Pott's *'History of Banbury'* records: "The first train left Banbury at 6.30 am when there was a large gathering of spectators but few passengers. There were more of both when the 9.45 am and 1.45 pm trains left for Bletchley, the neighbourhood of the station having the appearance of a fair, with flags, booths and stalls and a brass band. The last train of the day left at 5 pm."

Festivities were somewhat heightened when it was learned that the first message to be received upon the railway telegraph was the news of the birth of the Duke of Connaught.

Chapter Three

Banbury

The town of Banbury has enjoyed a fairly thriving economy for many centuries, it is believed that a market existed there in late Saxon times. Predominantly the basic trades have always been agricultural, it was also an important centre for wool in the 13th century. By the 18th century when the population was about 3000 people the town had established itself as a cloth weaving and dyeing centre (with the local worsted plush becoming quite famous) together with a prosperous cheese and leather trade, all of which was ably nourished by a thriving canal system; the main Oxford to Birmingham canal runs through the centre of the town.

Regarding railway progress, details of the political conflicts that preceded the lines adventure have been described in the first chapter, the story is now taken up from the point of view of the townspeople themselves. The Banbury Guardian reported the following in its issue of Thursday, 21st February, 1850 under the heading 'Buckinghamshire Railway'.

"The half-yearly meeting of this company was held on Thursday at the Euston station of the London and North Western Railway Company, Sir Harry Verney, M.P. in the chair.

Mr Watkin, the Secretary, read the report, which stated that £941,880 had been received and £933,597 spent for the purposes of the railway, leaving a balance of £8,253. "The works of the Banbury line are progressing rapidly to completion, and but for an unexpected delay in obtaining possession of the land for the station at Banbury the line might have been opened for traffic in March next." During this same meeting Mr Watkin in replying to questions from the Board stated that: "Stations on the line would be opened wherever the traffic would justify the expense. In the first instance the principal stations only would be opened." This last sentence would probably be referring to Buckingham, Brackley and Banbury. The newspaper goes on to report, "That a cordial vote of thanks was passed to the Rev. Freemantle for his zealous and gratuitous services in promoting the religious instruction for the men employed on the works."

An editorial leader contained within the same issue of this paper took a less convinced indeed slightly sarcastic attitude that the two railways were not proceeding with more haste. "On the Buckinghamshire, the permanent rails are laid to within about half-a-mile of Banbury, and the locomotive may now be seen daily traversing up to that point. We observe, it was stated at the general meeting of the shareholders in this line, last week, that the line will be opened to the public on the first of May. The only thing that would lead us to doubt this is, that, as yet, there is no station at Banbury, and no appearance of any erection that might serve for one; and although we are told that this is to be temporary and a wooden one, still the age of magic is past, and a *wooden* erection of the extent which would be required, is not to be expected up in a night like a mushroom, or as speedily as Cinderella's pumpkin was turned into a coach."

One interesting footnote, when the railways were built Banbury lost its racecourse, the site being purchased by the companies for their stations.

When the two lines were opened, almost together, the town's economy was given a new impetus. As a result of the conflicting ambitions of the two largest railway companies of the day the town happily inherited their desires to absorb all its trade, whilst the canal boat owners approached raw times. This increase in prosperity becomes further evident by the expansion of a new bank under Joseph Ashby Gillet and his successors.

Conveyance in the new form of transport was not without risk in those early days as this cutting from the Oxford Herald of 1852, describing the fate of Mr Golby's butter on the new railway bears witness:

> **BANBURY.** *Nov. 1862*
> Lately died, at Paris, Lieut.-General Sir Chas. Doyle, G.C.B.
> Sir Charles's second son is Lieut.Colonel John Sidney North,
> now of Wroxton, in this county, who married Lady Susan,
> second _____
> subsequently took the name and arms of North.
>
> FIRE—On Monday, as the luggage train which conveys goods from Banbury was on its way to London, the sparks from the engine set fire to one of the waggons, and Mr. Golby's immense load of butter being soon converted into melted butter, a large quantity of goods from Banbury and elsewhere were speedily fried and baked: we have not heard the amount of the loss, but believe it to have been considerable.
>
> STYNING.—We understand that Mr. R.J. Edward

No. *4 8*

BUCKINGHAM AND BRACKLEY JUNCTION RAILWAY AND OXFORD AND BLETCHLEY JUNCTION RAILWAY COMPANIES' AMALGAMATION AND EXTENSION OF LINES.

(Branches or Extensions to Banbury, Aylesbury and into Oxford, with Power to the London and North Western Railway Company to amalgamate with or subscribe to, or to purchase or lease the undertaking.)

BANBURY EXTENSION.

23rd November, 1846.

Sir,

We beg to inform you that application is intended to be made to Parliament in the ensuing Session, for an Act to authorize and empower the union and consolidation into one undertaking, of the Oxford and Bletchley Junction Railway Company and the Buckingham and Brackley Junction Railway Company, and to enable the Company so to be consolidated to make extension or Branch Railways to Banbury and Aylesbury, and a Branch Railway or Deviation in or near the City of Oxford, and that the Property mentioned in the annexed Schedule, or some part thereof, in which we understand you are interested, as therein stated, will be required for the purposes of the said Undertaking, according to the Lines thereof, as at present laid out, or may be required to be taken, under the usual powers of deviation, which will be applied for in the said Act, to the extent shewn or defined on the Plans hereinafter mentioned, and which property will be passed through in the manner mentioned in such Schedule.

We also beg to inform you that Plans and Sections of the said Undertaking, with Books of Reference thereto, have been or will be deposited with the several Clerks of the Peace of the Counties of Northampton, Oxford, and Buckingham, on or before the 30th day of November, 1846; and that copies of so much of the said Plans and Sections as relate to the Parish in which your Property is situate, with a Book of Reference thereto, have been or will be deposited for public inspection, with the Clerk of the said Parish, on or before the 30th day of November, 1846, on which Plan your Property is designated, by the numbers set forth in the annexed Schedule.

As we are required to report to Parliament whether you assent to, or dissent from the proposed Undertaking, or whether you are neuter in respect thereto, you will oblige us by writing your answer of assent, dissent or neutrality, in the form left herewith, and returning the same to us, with your Signature, on or before the 21st day of December, 1846, and if there should be any error or misdescription in the annexed Schedule, we shall feel obliged by your informing us thereof at your earliest convenience, that we may correct the same without delay.

We are,

Your obedient Servants,

PARKER, HAYES, BARNWELL AND TWISDEN,
1, Lincoln's Inn Fields, London,

SAM^L. CARTER, Birmingham,

Solicitors for the Bill.

To *The Trustees of the Banbury and Lutterworth Turnpike Road Edmund Finger Burton Daventry*

One hopes that passengers were spared the inflammable atmosphere at Banbury as the fare prices of the day were not modest even by 19th century standards, shortly after opening they were as follows: First Class to London 14s. 0d. (70p); Second 10s. 3d. (51½p); Third 7s. 0d. (35p) with return tickets at a quarter to two thirds extra. From Banbury to Brackley the single fares were 6d.(2½p), 4d. (2p) and 3d. (1½p) and to Buckingham 1s. 0d. (5p), 6d. and 4d. The Buckinghamshire Railway were able to reduce the price of coal to the inhabitants of the town from 22s. 0d. (£1.10p) to 15s. 0d. (75p) per ton on a requirement of 150,000 tons per annum.

One name that can be regarded as something of a founder of Banbury industry in the 19th century is that of Sir Bernhard Samuelson who developed the famous Britannia Foundry in 1848 after being forced to abandon his railway works at Tours, following the French Revolution. The foundry produced the farm machinery that was very much in demand all over the world at that time; this included the famous Banbury Turnip Cutter invented by John Gardner, a local townsman who founded the works which were the basis of the Britannia Foundry. Continuing in this tradition the produce of Samuelson's were built to a very high standard and the essential link in the firm's future prosperity undoubtedly depended upon the arrival of the railways. Once this was achieved expansion was rapid and it was this company (with its two foot gauge railway of wagons drawn by horses through the streets of the town to link the factory to the two railheads) that was responsible for transforming some of the local workforce from an agrarian to an industrial population. In 1859 Bernhard Samuelson became Banbury's M.P. and in 1884 after the works had turned out 8,000 reaping machines in a single year he was made a Baronet. During these busy years that lasted well into the twentieth century it was not considered extraordinary for the unpainted machines to be loaded onto the train along with a squad of painters who would perform this task whilst the cargo was en route! The climax of this prosperity was reached during the first world war after which sales began to fall; it was a decline that could not be arrested and the slump of 1931 dealt the body blow that finished the company in 1933.

The Britannia Foundry was not alone in its success, however. Another company that started production from its Vulcan Foundry in 1837 was the firm of Lampitt and Co. The Lampitt's seemed to represent that Victorian characteristic of inventiveness that flourished even in the backwaters of industrial life. In 1847 Charles Lampitt produced a mobile steam engine whilst John Lampitt invented systems of two- and three-speed gearing for traction engines, they also supplied the huge steam engine for the brewery at Hook Norton, a device that is still in use today.

At the Great Exhibition of 1851 the small town of Banbury was represented by two of the liveliest farm machinery producers of the day,

Rusher's Directory, Banbury — 1851

Banbury Library

a horse-seed-driller was exhibited by Charles Lampitt, with a significant
display of the latest in farm machinery from the Britannia Works, some
of which began their journeys all over the world from the branch.

Referring to the plans of the L.N.W.R. station it will be noticed that
two grain sidings were installed next to the goods shed. This was probably due, or at least in part to the fact that Mr Thomas Hunt had decided
to expand his already thriving brewery by moving into the new larger
premises of an old malt house in Bridge Street, once owned by John
Hunt. This was in 1847 and as the Banburian thirst was so consistent he
was aided still further in building up the business by receiving the
partnership of William Edmunds in 1850, becoming known as 'Hunt,
Edmunds.' By 1866 the brewery was supplying a large area of the South
Midlands.

Thus the town continued to prosper with every advantage of the new
railways, both of which were required to lay in new sidings to accommodate the traffic. There was also a lighter side to the developments at
Banbury; at the Banbury Fair of 1858 the L.N.W.R. brought 1,000
passengers into the festivities along the branch, with excursions to

Good photograph taken from the northern gasholder in 1931. On the left is the now closed L.N.W.R. m.p.d. whilst the Great Western depot flourishes in the distant fields. In the foreground a G.W.R. wagon stands on the entrance and recovery line on that Company's side.

Taken from the southern gasholder in 1931. The distant town of Banbury is on the left with the G.W.R. goods shed, on the extreme right is the L.N.W.R. goods shed and a fragmentary view of the station. The 'Banbury Gas & Coke' wagons are standing on the L.N.W.R. entrance and recovery section.

Banbury Gas Co.

London in the same year. In 1851 and 1852 promenade concerts were held at both stations with planking arranged across the tracks, whilst the ticket offices served as refreshment rooms.

In this summary of Banbury industries that directly owe their prosperity to the building of the railways there still remains one very distinct omission and that is the Banbury Gas and Coke Company who became integrated with both lines in the town for over a hundred years. The original site of this company was on the side of the Oxford Canal in Bridge Street. In 1850 the Buckinghamshire Railway put out an invitation to tender for the supply of seventy gas lights; the Banbury Gas Company's tender was successful and the lamps were duly installed. By 1854 the gas company decided that a much larger gas producing complex would be required to meet the needs of the rapidly expanding town and for the purpose of building the new plant a site was purchased from a Mr Tomlin of London, this was the area between the two running lines of railways which enabled a very convenient integration. In 1857 the new Works was in production and coal was brought in along a special siding that ran through the Works and connected the two railway companies in the same manner as the exchange siding was to do several years later. Deliveries were twice a week and as locomotives were not allowed into the gasworks itself the wagons had to be winched along the rails by means of a device called a steam-crab and wire rope. Before the exchange siding was built this must have proved awkward as the eventual working method was to return wagons to their respective companies along this connection. Inside the Works the coal was unloaded direct into an underground hopper, thence to a coal-breaker via an elevator to the hopper of the stoking machine. When graded coal was introduced the coal-breaker was removed but the remainder of the system operated like this until the works closed in 1958. Today a single holder contains north sea gas and much of the remaining buildings belong to a local scrap merchant.

In the 1850's it became obvious that the South Midlands were destined to become an industrial area, new factories were being built in many of the towns including Banbury which was now well situated with direct rail and canal access. It became apparent at this time that the large deposits of smelting ore at Wroxton would soon be worked out placing a greater importance on the plentiful supply that still existed in Northampton, thus creating the stimulus for another railway company in the area. This company was called the Northampton and Banbury Railway which obtained powers to construct a line from Blisworth to run south and join the Buckinghamshire line at Cockley Brake between Brackley and Banbury. Parliamentary sanction was first received in 1847, at that time the intention was for it to be leased by the L.N.W.R. but the project lapsed. The next time that it reappeared was in July 1863, the fresh act being suffixed with the word 'Junction.' One other rather novel proposal of 1864 avoided joining the Banbury branch at all save in the

GREAT WESTERN RAILWAY.
EASTER HOLIDAYS.
EXCURSION TO LONDON AND BACK.

On *EASTER MONDAY, April the* 13*th,*

AN EXCURSION TRAIN will leave BANBURY STATION at 7.15, a.m., for LONDON, and will return from Paddington Station at 6.30, p.m., the same day.

FARES (THERE AND BACK):—
FIRST-CLASS, 8s.; COVERED CARRIAGES, 5s.

Tickets are not transferable, and are available only by the Trains above indicated.

Children, under Twelve years of age, Half-price.

LONDON & NORTH WESTERN RAILWAY.
EASTER HOLIDAYS.
A CHEAP EXCURSION TRAIN

WILL LEAVE BANBURY FOR LONDON,
On *EASTER MONDAY, April* 13.

Leave BANBURY	7.30, a.m.	
„ BRACKLEY	7.50	„
„ BUCKINGHAM	8. 5	„
„ WINSLOW	8 20	„
Arrive at LONDON	10.30	„

RETURNING from the Euston Square Station the same Evening, by Special Train, at Seven o'clock. Passengers desirous of proceeding to Fenchurch Street, for the City, can alight at the Camden Town Station, whence the North London Trains start every 15 minutes,

There will be no extra charge for continuing on to Fenchurch Street, but Passengers must join the Return Train at the Euston Square Station.

FARES FOR THE DOUBLE JOURNEY:—

	First Class.	Covered Carriages.
BANBURY	**8s.**	**5s.**
BRACKLEY ⎫ BUCKINGHAM ⎭	**6s. 6d.**	**4s.**

☞ Children, under Twelve years of age, Half-price.

Competing interests at Banbury on Thursday, 9th April, 1857.

Banbury Guardian

station itself. This plan deviated north from a point roughly mid-way between Wappenham and Helmdon, describing an arc that brought the line into the town from the north in a similar manner to that of the Great Central Woodford Halse line some years later, passing through the town to connect with the L.N.W.R. in the station. This revived the old spectre of a through station again, this time to Northampton, but nothing came of this plan. Although running powers were granted by the L.N.W.R. for this railway to run along the remaining five and a half miles of the branch into Banbury the L.N.W.R. felt that as it was a single line the Northampton and Banbury would eventually be obliged to lay a separate set of rails alongside; fortunately for the latter the L.N.W.R. never pressed them in this matter. Consequently this section of the N & B was the only constructed permanent way of a much greater and ambitious project. As I have already mentioned the basis of this railway was founded on the iron ore deposits of the Northampton area. If this could be directly connected by rail to the blast furnaces in South Wales the results could be a thriving concern for railway investors which indeed was a sound basis for the line. In all, when connected with the blast furnaces of Dowlais and Ebbw Vale there would be ninety six and a half miles of line to be known as the Midland Counties and South Wales Railway. To this effect the company began to promote the next part of the line from Banbury to Blockley; this venture did not go without opposition as another company, the Chipping Norton & Banbury Railway was also formed to propose that the next line from Banbury should be from the village of Chipping Norton linking with the Oxon-Banbury line at Kings Sutton. Originally the argument as to which company should be entitled to span this area of the Cotswolds had started some time before, in 1858, when the opposing factions held a meeting in Banbury Town Hall. A John Collister, who along with Charles Liddell drew up the plans for the N&B, read a statement on behalf of that company as follows: "The Banbury-Blockley Station on the West Midland section of the GWR and run in an easterly path to the town of Banbury, where it would form a junction with the Buckingham branch of the LNWR near the existing Banbury station of the latter company, with a connection with the GWR this would of course bring the Northamptonshire iron and South Wales coal mines into direct communication". Whatever became of the 1858 wrangle is not clear but a map belonging to a prospective shareholder of the Chipping Norton to Banbury line shows some interesting routes inked in, the date on this map is 1865. The routes delineated show the N&B leaving the Bucking-hamshire line at a junction where the line curves into the Cherwell valley and carrying on to Bloxham. At the latter place one line continues on towards Blockley whilst the other turns southward to reach Chipping Norton. It is a fact that the Chipping Norton line was not built until 1887 whereas the fate of the N&B venture was decided by an unsuspected blow from foreign parts. During the 1860's Spain began to export a

RAILWAY TIME TABLES, NOVEMBER, 1868.

LONDON AND NORTH-WESTERN.

FROM BANBURY.

Dis. Mls	STATIONS. Leave	WEEK DAYS. A.M.	A.M.	P.M.	P.M.	P.M.	SUN P.M.
	BANBURY	7 55	9 10	12 55	4 0	7 20	2 40
4	Farthinghoe	8 2	9 17	1 2	4 7	7 27	2 51
9¾	Brackley	8 15	9 30	1 15	4 20	7 40	3 6
17	Buckingham	8 28	9 43	1 30	4 33	7 53	3 22
21¾	Verney Junction	8 39	..	1 44	4 44	..	..
23¾	Winslow	8 45	10 0	1 50	4 50	8 10	3 39
25¾	Swanbourne	9 0	..	..	..	8 27	3 47
31¼	Bletchley, (*Junc.*)	9 13	10 25	2 25	5 10	8 40	4 0
78	LONDON	10 30	12 15	4 0	8 10	10 40	6 25
47½	Bedford	10 25	1 0	3 20	6 25	9 50	..
47½	Blisworth	10 18	11 12	3 38	6 10	10 40	..
52½	Northampton	10 3	11 40	3 55	6 20	9 50	..
54½	Weedon	10 49	11 25	3 53	6 24	..	..
67¼	Rugby	11 0	11 50	4 30	6 45	11 10	..
78½	Coventry	12 13	12 25	5 26	7 40	11 40	..
97	BIRMINGHAM	12 5	1 0	6 5	8 10	12 15	..
182	Manchester	2 0	3 0	7 45	10 0	2 45	..
194¾	Liverpool	2 30	3 30	8 15	10 30	3 20	..

The 7.55 A.M Train from Banbury takes 3rd Class Passengers to and from Stations between Banbury and Bletchley, to the North by the 7.45 a.m. London Train from Bletchley, & to the Bedford Branch and Stations up to Cambridge.

The 9.10 A.M. Train from Banbury takes 3rd Class Passengers to the South.

The 4.0 P.M. Train from Banbury takes 3rd Class Passengers from Banbury to London only.

The 7.20 P.M. Train from Banbury conveys 3rd Class Passengers to Stations between Winslow and Oxford.

TO BANBURY.

Dis Mls.	STATIONS. Leave	WEEK DAYS. A.M.	A.M.	P.M.	P.M.	P.M.	SUN A.M.
78	LONDON	6 25	11 0	1 0	3 30	6 15	10 0
194¾	Liverpool	..	..	9 0	11 30	..	..
182	Manchester	..	6 10	9 30	12 0	..	..
97	BIRMINGHAM	..	9 30	12 25	2 7	4 0	8 30
78½	Coventry	..	10 4	..	2 27	4 34	9 20
67¼	Rugby	..	10 48	1 45	3 35	5 7	10 2
54½	Weedon	..	10 58	..	2 28	5 36	10 37
52½	Northampton	7 15	10 47	2 20	3 50	5 38	10 40
47½	Bedford	7 15	11 10	2 40	4 37	7 23	10 16
47½	Blisworth	7 35	11 12	..	2 45	5 52	10 38
31¼	Bletchley, (*Junc.*)	8 25	12 20	3 30	5 20	8 20	11 50
25¾	Swanbourne	8 35	..	3 43	5 30	8 31	12 1
23¾	Winslow	8 55	12 45	3 55	5 35	8 41	12 7
21¾	Verney Junction	9 0	12 50	..	5 40	..	..
17	Buckingham	9 11	1 0	4 33	5 51	8 57	12 23
9¾	Brackley	9 30	1 15	4 50	6 8	9 14	12 40
4	Farthinghoe	9 43	1 30	5 5	6 23	9 29	12 55
	BANBURY	9 55	1 45	5 17	6 35	9 41	1 7

The 12.15 noon Train from Bletchley takes 3rd Class Passengers to Banbury from all Stations between Wolverhampton and London.

The 3.30 P.M Train from London takes 3rd Class Passengers from London to Banbury only.

FROM BANBURY TO OXFORD.

Dis. Miles.	STATIONS.	WEEK DAYS A. M.	A. M.	A. M.	P. M.	P. M.	P. M.	SUN. P. M.
	Banbury	7 55	9 10	..	12 55	4 0	7 20	..
4	Farthinghoe	8 2	9 17	..	1 2	4 7	7 27	..
9¾	Brackley	8 15	9 30	..	1 15	4 20	7 40	..
17	Buckingham	8 28	9 43	..	1 30	4 33	7 53	..
21¾	Verney Junction	8 39	..	..	1 44	4 44	..	..
23¾	Winslow.... *Arrive*	8 45	10 0	..	1 50	4 50	8 10	..
	Leave	8 52	11 0	12 40	3 50	5 55	9 22	12 1
	Verney Junction	8 57	..	12 45	..	6 0	..	..
27¾	Claydon	9 4	11 10	12 50	4 5	6 5	9 38	..
33¾	Launton	9 17	..	..	4 18	..	..	..
36	Bicester	9 23	11 25	1 5	4 24	6 20	9 53	12 29
42¾	Islip	9 35	11 38	1 18	4 36	6 33	10 6	12 43
47¾	Oxford	9 50	11 50	1 30	4 50	6 45	10 20	12 55

FROM OXFORD TO BANBURY.

Dis. Mls.	STATIONS.	WEEK DAYS. A. M.	A. M.	NOON.	P. M.	P. M.	P. M.	SUN A. M.
	Oxford	8 0	9 15	1 15	4 15	5 15	7 30	10 0
5	Islip	8 11	9 25	1 25	4 25	5 25	7 40	10 11
11¾	Bicester	8 25	9 38	1 38	4 38	5 38	7 53	10 26
14	Launton	..	9 43	..	..	..	7 58	..
20	Claydon	8 41	9 54	1 53	4 54	5 55	8 10	10 44
22	Verney Junction	8 46	..	1 57	..	5 58	..	..
24	Winslow....*Arrive*	8 50	10 3	2 2	5 2	6 2	8 17	10 56
	Leave	..	12 45	3 55	5 35	..	8 37	12 7
	Verney Junction	9 0	12 50	..	5 40	..	..	..
30¾	Buckingham	9 11	1 0	4 33	5 51	..	8 57	12 23
38	Brackley	9 30	1 15	4 50	6 8	..	9 1[illegible]	12 40
43¾	Farthinghoe	9 43	1 30	5 5	6 23	..	9 29	12 55
47¾	Banbury	9 55	1 45	5 17	6 35	..	9 41	1 7

Time Table, 1868

Banbury Guardian

BANBURY TO BLETCHLEY, OXFORD, AND AYLESBURY.

	WEEK DAYS.								SUN.	
STATIONS.	a.m.	a.m.	p.m.	p.m.	p.m.	p.m.	p.m.	p.m.	a.m.	p.m.
BANBURY	7 35	9 50	...	...	2 15	4 0	7 15	...	7 35	4 15
Farthinghoe	8 22	9 58	...	...	2 23	4 7	7 23	...	...	4 26
Brackley	8 14	10 10	...	...	2 35	4 20	7 40	...	...	4 41
Westbury Crossing	8 22	10 18	...	...	2 43	4 28	7 48	...	...	4 49
Buckingham	8 29	10 28	...	...	2 53	4 37	7 57	6 40	...	4 57
Padbury	8 43	10 41	...	...	3 1	4 44	8 4	...	...	5 5
Verney Junction	8 43	10 41	...	...	3 7	4 50	8 11	6 52	...	5 11
Quainton Road	9 4	11 4	...	...	...	5 45	...	...	...	...
Aylesbury	9 18	11 20	...	...	...	6 0	...	...	...	...
Winslow	8 50	10 46	...	...	3 13	4 35	8 17	7 0	...	5 16
Winslow	8 47	10 32	12 38	...	4 14	4 52	9 26	11 51	...	...
Verney Junction	8 55	10 23	12 46	...	4 53	6 7	...	...	...	...
Claydon	8 59	10 46	12 52	...	5 0	7 5	9 40	12 3	...	...
Marsh Gibbon and Poundon	5 10	10 12	12 58	...	5 6	7 11	...	12 9	...	...
Launton	9 10	...	...	...	...	...	...	...	...	...
Bicester	9 15	11 14	1 10	...	5 21	7 28	9 58	12 19	...	...
Islip	9 27	11 16	1 23	...	5 35	7 35	10 10	12 33	...	...
Oxford	9 40	11 30	1 35	...	5 50	7 50	10 25	12 45	...	...
Swanbourne	...	...	...	...	...	5 3	8 34	7 8	...	5 25
Bletchley	9 11	11 12	...	...	3 26	5 14	8 45	7 20	3 40	5 37

* For Horse Boxes and Milk only. § Calls to set down on notice being given by the Passengers to the Guard at the preceding stopping Station, and to pick up Passengers.

BLETCHLEY, OXFORD, AND AYLESBURY TO BANBURY.

	WEEK DAYS.								SUN.	
STATIONS.	a.m.	a.m.	a.m.	p.m.	p.m.	p.m.	p.m.	p.m.	a.m.	p.m.
Bletchley	8 36	...	10 15	12 20	...	2 30	6 30	9 10	5 45	11 40
Swanbourne	8 41	...	...	§	...	4 46	6 41	...	...	11 51
Oxford	7 50	9 0	10 0	12 0	...	2 30	4 35	7 30	...	9 15
Islip	8 0	9 10	10 11	...	...	4 45	4 45	7 40	...	9 26
Bicester	8 12	9 19	10 24	12 19	...	2 53	4 58	7 54	...	9 41
Launton	8 19	...	...	...	...	§	...	8 2	...	...
Marsh Gibbon and Poundon	8 24	...	10 31	...	...	3 1	5 7	8 8	...	9 51
Claydon	8 33	...	10 39	12 37	...	3 13	5 15	8 16	...	9 59
Verney Junction	8 40	...	10 45	12 42	...	3 20	5 28	...	...	...
Winslow	8 46	9 40	10 52	...	...	3 26	5 28	8 24	...	10 11
Winslow	8 47	...	...	10 32	12 38	4 51	6 46	9 26	6 0	11 57
Aylesbury	7 50	...	...	11 51	...	3 55	...	...	...	...
Quainton Road	8 5	...	...	12 6	...	4 9	...	...	...	...
Verney Junction	8 57	...	...	10 50	12 48	4 58	6 52	...	6 20	...
Padbury	9 4	...	...	10 12	12 55	5 5	6 58	...	...	...
Buckingham	9 11	10 55	...	11 10	1 11	5 12	7 5	9 51	6 32	12 8
Westbury Crossing	9 17	11 5	...	11 17	1 11	5 17	7 17	...	...	12 16
Brackley	9 26	11 12	...	11 23	1 19	5 28	7 34	9 10 2	...	12 26
Farthinghoe	9 38	11 25	...	1 31	1 31	5 40	7 42	...	...	12 33
BANBURY	9 45	11 35	...	1 40	1 40	5 48	10 25	...	1 0	12 50

† Thursday only.

RUGBY TO STAMFORD & PETERBOROUGH.

	a.m.	a.m.	a.m.	p.m.	p.m.	p.m.	p.m.	p.m.	Sun.	
									a.m.	p.m.
Rugby	8 30	9 20	10 50	12 55	5 10	5 57	10	5 55	7 10	7 35
Market Harbro'	9 15	9 55	11 21	1 40	5 41	6 40	7 55	...	...	8 20
Seaton	9 46	...	11 49	2 18	6 7	7 11	8 40	...	...	...
Seaton	9 50	...	11 50	2 25	6 10	7 12	8 45	...	...	...
Stamford	10 15	...	12 10	2 50	6 30	7 35	9 6	...	...	...
Seaton	9 47	...	11 52	2 19	6 8	...	8 42	...	...	...
Peterborough	10 35	...	12 33	3 10	6 45	...	9 30	...	...	...

PETERBOROUGH & STAMFORD TO RUGBY.

	a.m.	a.m.	a.m.	p.m.	p.m.	p.m.	p.m.	Sun.	
								a.m.	p.m.
Peterborough	8 30	10 30	12 10	1 55	...	...	6 20	...	...
Seaton	9 19	11 7	12 46	2 46	...	...	7 2	...	...
Stamford	7 0	8 50	10 35	12 20	2 20	...	6 40	...	...
Seaton	7 23	9 15	11 0	12 44	2 44	...	7 4	...	...
Seaton	7 24	9 21	11 1	12 47	2 47	...	7 6	...	...
Market Harbro'	8 15	10 5	11 37	1 18	3 25	5 45	7 35	6 0	...
Rugby	9 10	10 37	12 15	1 54	4 15	6 30	8 10	6 45	...

NORTHAMPTON TO RUGBY.

	a.m.	a.m.	p.m.	p.m.	p.m.	p.m.	p.m.	p.m.
Northampton, Castle St	8 15	11 57	2 25	4 47	6 14	8 10	...	...
Althorp Park	8 30	12 12	2 40	5 1	6 22	8 25	...	...
Long Buckby	8 39	12 19	2 49	5 8	6 32	8 34	...	...
Kilsby and Crick	8 52	12 29	3 2	5 17	6 41	8 47	...	...
Rugby	9 0	12 57	3 10	5 25	6 47	8 55	...	...

RUGBY TO NORTHAMPTON.

	a.m.	a.m.	p.m.	p.m.	p.m.	p.m.	p.m.	p.m.
Rugby	7 10	10 33	1 25	3 35	5 25	8 35	...	...
Kilsby and Crick	7 18	10 41	1 32	3 43	5 46	8 43	...	...
Long Buckby	7 31	10 51	1 42	3 56	5 56	8 56	...	...
Althorp Park	7 40	10 58	1 49	4 3	7 6	9 5	...	...
Northampton, Castle St	7 55	11 13	2 3	4 19	6 10	9 20	...	...

BLETCHLEY TO LONDON.

	a.m.	a.m.	p.m.	p.m.	p.m.	Sun.	
						a.m.	p.m.
Bletchley	9 26	11 24	2 0	5 8	9 0	7 30	5 40
Leighton	10 6	12 15	51 4	30 7	4 9 15	7 42	5 52
Dunstable	10 55	12 30	3 15	5 17	30 9 35	...	...
Cheddington	10 19	12 25	2 4	5 7	21 9 26	7 53	6 15
Aylesbury	10 50	12 45	30 5	50 7 45	...	...	...
Watford	11 25	1 20	3 45	5 54	8 12	10 15	...
St. Albans	11 42	1 43	3 32	9 42	...	10 15	...
London	10 35	12 52	30 4	50 7	30 10 10 5	...	...

LONDON TO BLETCHLEY.

	a.m.	a.m.	p.m.	p.m.	p.m.	Sun.	
						a.m.	p.m.
London	7 15	9 0	11 0	3 0	5 15	8 9	10 0
St. Albans	...	9 10	10 30	2 54	5 7	5 9	10 0
Watford	6 52	9 31	10 47	2 40	53 7 35	...	10 34
Aylesbury	7 58	25	11 10	4 0	10 8 10	...	10 49
Cheddington	7 36	9 49	11 30	3 18	28	...	10 19
Dunstable	6 55	8 17	11 20	2 50	8 20 8 15	...	...
Leighton	7 47	9 20	11 51	3 21	41 8 37	...	10 28
Bletchley	8 21	10 11	12 6	4 8	6 22 9 6	...	11 12

London & North Western Railway time-table appearing in the *Banbury Guardian* on 12th July, 1883.

Banbury and London (Euston).—L. & N. W. R.

Stations.	a.m.	a.m.	p.m.	p.m.	p.m.	p.m.	Sundays a.m.	Sundays p.m.
BANBURY	**7 40**	**9 50**	**2 20**	**4 25**	**7 15**	...	...	**4 15**
Farthinghoe	7 47	9 58	2 28	4 33	7 23	...	...	4 26
Brackley	7 58	10 10	2 40	4 45	7 40	...	...	4 41
Fulwell & Westbry	8 7	10 18	2 46	4 53	7 48	...	...	4 49
Buckingham	8 14	10 28	2 56	5 1	7 57	...	6 40	4 57
Padbury	8 22	10 35	3 2	5 9	8 5	...	6 46	5 5
Verney Junct. ..	8 28	10 41	3 6	5 15	8 11	...	6 52	5 11
Winslow .... arr.	8 36	10 46	3 11	5 20	8 17	...	7 0	5 16
Quainton Road	8 54	...	...	5 45	...	...	...	...
Aylesbury	9 8	...	...	6 0	...	...	...	...
Swanbourne	8 44	10 55	...	5 30	8 30	...	7 8	5 25
Bletchley....arr.	**8 55**	**11 6**	**3 28**	**5 42**	**8 40**	...	**7 20**	**5 37**
Leighton	9 46	12 9	3 53	6 33	9 20	...	7 42	5 52
Dunstable	10 45	12 30	5 0	7 30	9 40	...	...	...
Aylesbury	10 50	12 45	5 55	7 12	...	...	8 20	...
Watford	10 49	1 20	5 0	7 35	10 25	...	8 41	7 4
St. Albans	11 42	1 45	5 42	7 57	...	...	9 55	8 5
Willesden........	9 52	12 15	4 45	6 58	10 0	...	9 10	7 38
Euston	**10 5**	**12 30**	**5 0**	**7 10**	**10 15**	...	**9 35**	**8 10**

Stations.	a.m.	a.m. (Thursdays only.)	a.m.	a.m.	p.m.	p.m.	p.m.	Sundays a.m.
Euston	**7 15**	...	**9 0**	**11 0**	**3 0**	**5 15**	**7 0**	**10 0**
Willesden........	6 18	...	9 12	11 12	3 12	5 27	7 12	10 12
St. Albans	...	...	9 15	10 30	2 0	4 5	7 5	10 10
Watford	6 50	...	9 31	10 47	2 35	4 51	7 37	10 35
Aylesbury	7 5	...	9 10	11 10	2 15	4 15	8 10	10 0
Dunstable	6 55		9 38	11 25	1 40	4 7	8 15	...
Leighton	7 47		9 55	11 45	3 24	5 44	8 37	10 28
Bletchley .. dep.	**8 25**		**10 15**	**12 20**	**4 25**	**6 32**	**9 10**	**11 40**
Swanbourne	8 36		...	...	4 36	6 43	...	11 51
Winslow	8 42		10 32	12 38	4 41	6 48	9 26	11 57
Aylesbury	7 50		...	11 51	3 55	...	...	...
Quainton Road	8 5		...	12 6	4 9	...	...	...
Verney Junct. dep	8 52	*	10 50	12 48	4 48	6 54	...	...
Padbury	8 59	...	11 0	12 55	4 55	7 0	...	12 8
Buckingham	9 6	*10*55*	11 15	1 2	5 2	7 7	9 51	12 16
Fulwell & Westbry	9 12	*11 5*	11 23	1 11	5 11	7 13	...	12 26
Brackley	9 21	*11 12*	11 35	1 19	5 18	7 20	10 2	12 33
Farthinghoe	9 33	*11 25*	...	1 31	5 30	7 34	...	12 50
BANBURY	**9 40**	*11*35*	...	**1 40**	**5 38**	**7 42**	**10 25**	**1 0**

Banbury and Oxford.—L. & N. W. R.

Stations.	a.m.	a.m.	p.m.	p.m.	p.m.
BANBURY	**7 40**	**9 50**	**2 20**	**4 25**	**7 15**
Verney Junct	8 28	10 41	3 6	5 15	8 11
Claydon	8 54	10 48	5 0	6 52	9 40
Marsh Gibbn	9 0	10 54	5 6	6 58	...
Launton	9 5	...	...	...	...
Bicester	9 10	11 4	5 21	7 10	9 58
Islip	9 22	11 16	5 35	7 23	10 10
Oxford	**9 35**	**11 30**	**5 50**	**7 40**	**10 25**

Stations.	a.m.	p.m.	p.m.	p.m.	p.m.	Sundays a.m.
Oxford	**7 40**	**12 10**	**2 30**	**4 35**	**7 30**	**9 15**
Islip	7 50	...	2 40	4 45	7 40	9 26
Bicester	8 2	12 29	2 53	4 58	7 54	9 41
Launton	8 8	...	...	...	8 0	...
Marsh Gibbn	8 13	...	3 1	5 7	8 7	9 51
Claydon	8 21	...	3 9	5 15	8 15	9 59
Verney Junct	8 52	12 48	4 48	6 54	...	...
BANBURY	**9 40**	**1 40**	**5 38**	**7 40**	**10 25**	**1 0**

Banbury, the North and East, via Bletchley.—L. & N. W. and G. E.

Stations.	Week Days a.m.	a.m.	p.m.	p.m.	p.m.	... (* Via Leighton.)	Sun. p.m.
BANBURY	**7 40**	**9 50**	**2 20**	**4 25**	**7 15**	...	**4 15**
Bletchley	8 55	11 6	3 28	5 42	8 40	...	5 37
Bletchley ....dep.	10 14	11 19	3 50	6 11	8 50		*5*40*
Northampton	10 40	11 52	4 31	6 50	9 20		6 32
Rugby	11 12	12 5	4 40	7 0	10 0		7 0
Coventry	11 42	1 28	5 21	7 45	11 47		7 36
Birmingham	12 20	1 28	5 55	8 18	12 25		8 15
Nuneaton	11 37	12 29	5 21	7 28	11 29	...	7 22
Leicester	...	2 5	6 7	8 48	...	...	8 15
Lichfield	12 5	1 20	6 16	8 20	12 21	...	...
Burton	12 40	2 45	6 40	9 4	...	...	...
Derby	1 0	3 5	7 5	9 28	...	...	...
Stafford..........	12 31	2 5	6 45	8 45	12 23	...	8 18
Shrewsbury	1 45	...	7 55	9 52	3 0	...	3 0
Crewe	1 11	1 48	6 16	8 49	1 2	...	8 58
Chester	2 0	2 50	7 15	9 21	12 31	...	9 50
Liverpool	**2 20**	**3 0**	**7 15**	**10 0**	**3 0**	...	**10 20**
Manchester	**2 20**	**2 40**	**7 15**	**9 45**	**2 35**	...	**10 0**
Leeds..	4 45	4 45	10 20	3 0	...	...	3 0
Preston	2 47	4 23	9 30	11 10	2 27	...	10 40
Carlisle..........	5 22	7 0	...	...	4 10	...	4 10
Edinburgh (Prin. St)	8 0	10 0	...	...	6 45	...	6 45
Glasgow (Central) ..	8 0	10 15	...	...	6 55	...	6 55
Bletchley ....dep.	10 20	11 28	4 20	6 15	9 10	...	...
Bedford	10 54	11 56	5 0	7 0	9 55	...	...
Cambridge	...	**1 5**	**6 15**	**8 15**	...	...	...
Great Eastern Newmarket......	...	2 8	7 18	10 2	...	...	...
Bury St. Edmunds	...	2 50	8 0	...	...	...	...
Ipswich	...	4 16	9 30	...	...	...	...
Hunstanton	...	3 50	9 7	...	...	...	...
Norwich	...	3 53	8 48	2 0	...	...	...
Lowestoft	...	5 23	10 3	...	...	...	...
Yarmouth	...	4 57	9 47	3 0	...	...	...

Stations.	Week Days a.m.	a.m.	a.m.	p.m.	p.m.	
Great Eastern Yarmouth	...	6 49	10 10	1 0	3 40	‡ Mondays excepted.
Lowestoft	...	*6§30*	9 55	12 40	3 27	
Norwich	...	7 35	11 10	2 7	4 40	
Hunstanton	...	7 25	10 52	1 52	4 25	
Ipswich	...	7 3	10 23	2 10	4 35	
Bury St. Edmunds	...	8 28	11 30	3 21	5 39	...
Newmarket	...	8 58	12 25	4 0	6 15	...
Cambridge	...	**10 20**	**1 55**	**4 40**	**7 0**	...
Bedford	7 30	11 19	2 58	5 41	8 3	...
Bletchley ......arr.	8 5	11 44	3 35	6 15	8 40	...
Glasgow (Central)..	9 5	...	...	...	10 0	§ Mondays only.
Edinburgh (Prin. St.)	9 10	...	...	...	10 0	
Carlisle..........	12 5	...	8 40	...	12 55	
Preston..........	2 30	5 50	11 15	...	3 20	
Leeds..........	...	...	9 30	11 30	2 30	
Manchester	...	**7 45**	**12 0**	**2 15**	**5 15**	
Liverpool	**2 35**	**7 20**	**12 0**	**2 5**	**5 5**	...
Chester..........	*2‡35*	7 25	12 0	2 0	5 25	...
Crewe	3 55	8 35	1 5	3 10	6 15	...
Shrewsbury	...	7 45	12 50	2 30	5 35	...
Stafford	*4‡33*	9 15	1 48	3 49	6 57	...
Derby	...	9 0	1 30	3 20	...	‖ Saturdays.
Burton	...	9 18	1 48	3 39	...	
Lichfield	...	9 45	2 12	4 12	4 37	
Leicester	...	8 25	12 40	3 0	6 20	
Nuneaton	5 22	10 25	2 45	4 41	7 44	
Birmingham	...	9 40	2 10	4 0	6 50	
Coventry	...	10 11	2 44	4 34	6 46	...
Rugby	5 50	10 52	3 15	5 7	8 11	...
Northampton	7 55	11 22	3 45	5 36	8 38	...
Bletchley	8 20	11 49	4 10	6 3	9 2	...
Bletchley	8 25	12 20	4 25	6 32	9 10	...
BANBURY	**9 40**	**1 40**	**5 38**	**7 42**	**10 25**	...

The well-known local printers Cheney & Sons, published this Railway Guide for 1888.

Cheney & Sons

Banbury, Northampton, Market Harboro', Newark, &c.—L.N.W.

STATIONS.	a.m.	a.m.	a.m.	p.m.	p.m.	p.m.
BANBURY	7*30	10*25				1 45
Northampton	9 15	11 40	12 50	2 20	4 40	5 10
Mkt. Harbro'	9 58	11 28	1 34	5 24	9	6 15
Mkt. Harb.dp.		11 35	1 55	5 45	6 30	
Stamford		12 40	2 50	6 30	10 8	
Ptrboro' (G.E.)		12 40	3 48	6 45	10 20	

Banbury, Northampton, and Peterborough.—L.N.W.

STATIONS.	a.m.	a.m.	p.m.	p.m.	p.m.	p.m.
BANBURY	7*30	10*25	2 20		6*5	
Northampton	9 20	12 37	4 37		6 55	12 40
Castle Ashby	9 38	1 23	4 45		7 7	
Wellingboro'	9 46	1 31	5 6		7 24	4 45
Ely	9 55	1 52	5 17		8 9	5 57
Ptrboro' (g. E.)ar.	10 7	1 53	5 29		8 50	
Peterboro' (dp.	10 26	1 25			8 45	6 15
Wansford (Sbsn.)	10 37	6	5 49		9 11	6 30
Oundle					9 24	
Peterboro' (G.E.)	12 50	1 43	7 55		9 45	6 52
Thrapston					9 57	
Higham Ferrers					10 3	
Ely	2 55				10 12	7 17
Norwich	5 13				2	7 26
Lowestoft					5	
Yarmouth	4 57	7	6 10	36		3 0

Slow trains also leave Northampton at 7 20 a.m. Week-days and 11 50 a.m. Sundays,
arriving at Peterborough at 9 3 a.m. and 1 40 p.m. respectively.
Slow trains also leave Peterborough at 10 42 a.m. Week-days and 8 35 a.m. Sundays,
arriving at Northampton at 12 25 p.m. and 10 27 p.m. respectively.
* Banbury via Blisworth.

Banbury, Northampton, and Rugby.—L. and N.W.

STATIONS.	a.m.	a.m.	a.m.	a.m.	p.m.	p.m.	p.m.	p.m.
BANBURY			10 25	10 35	2 20		4 25	6 5
Northampton	8 10	11 54	2 25	6 6	8 20		4 35	
Althorp Park	8 24	12 12	2 40	6 14	8 34		4 42	4 53
Long Buckby	8 32	12 12	2 49	6 22	8 42		4 51	5 1
Kilsby & Crick	8 42	12 22	3 3	6 32	8 52		5 0	5 15
Rugby	8 50	12 30	3 10	6 40	9 0		5 45	5 42

STATIONS.	a.m.	a.m.	a.m.	p.m.	p.m.	p.m.	p.m.	p.m.
Rugby	8 10	11 54	2 25		4 25	6 5		
Kilsby & Crick	8 27			4 12		6 30		
Long Buckby	8 38	10 18	1 17	3 34	4 58	5 11		
Althorp Park	8 46	10 25	1 44	3 41	5 5	5 15		
Northampton	9 0	10 41	1 58	3 56	5 20	5 30		
BANBURY		1 40		5 45	5 45	7 42		

Banbury, Wolverton, and Newport Pagnell.—L. and N.W.

STATIONS.	a.m.	a.m.	a.m.	p.m.	p.m.	p.m.	p.m.	p.m.
BANBURY		7 30	10 25	2 20		4 25	7 15	
Bletchley dep.	10 20	11 23	2 40	4 12	6 30	6 50	8 20	
Wolverton arr.	10 30	11 33	4 22	6 40	9		8 32	
Newport Pagnl.							8 34	

STATIONS.	a.m.	a.m.	a.m.	p.m.	p.m.	p.m.	p.m.	p.m.
Newpt. Pgnl.dep.			8	1 50	4 13	5 53	7 29	8 50
Wolverton dep.	15	5 12	35	6 48	9 10			
Bletchley arr.	11	5 12	12	4 7	7 0		9 22	
BANBURY		9 40	1 40		5 38		7 42	10 25

Banbury, Birmingham, Burton, Derby, and Nottingham.—L.N.W.

STATIONS.	a.m.	a.m.	a.m.	p.m.	p.m.	p.m.	p.m.	p.m.
BANBURY (g.w.)			9 22	12 17	2 17		3 25	5 59
B'ham (New St.) dep.	6 30		9 20	10 35	1 30	2 20	4 25	5 50
Walsall	7 0		9 51	11 10	1 55	2 40	5 0	5 53
Lichfield (City)	7 5		10 9	11 40	2 17	3 0	5 20	7 42
Burton	8 40		10 54	12 40	2 45	3 40	6 16	6 40
Derby arr.	9 0		10 0		2 55	4 0	6 40	7 5

STATIONS.	a.m.	a.m.	a.m.	p.m.	p.m.	p.m.	p.m.	p.m.
Nottngham (Mid.)		6 55	8 15		9 22	10 0		11 10
Derby		7 15	8 40		9 18	11 43		9 10
Derby (L.N.w.) dep.		7 50	9 10		9 46	2 10		9 40
Burton		8 30	9 35		10 24	12 30		9 22
Lichfield (City)		9	10 45		12 58			11 25
B'ham (New St.) arr.		10 3	12		1 19			
BANBURY (g.w.)		11 25			1 19			3 20

Banbury, Liverpool, Manchester, Birmingham, London, &c.—L.N.W.

STATIONS.	a.m.	a.m.	a.m.	a.m.	p.m.	p.m.	noon
BANBURY	7 30	7*37	8 55		6 5		12 0
Farthinghoe*	7*37	10*32	11 45		6*12		12 5
Helmdon	7 52	10 47	9 1		6 27		12 10
Wappenham	8 4	10 59	9 22		6 39		4 5
Towcester	8 22	11 15	10 15		6 52		4 15
Blisworth	8 37	11 30	10 45		7 25		6 30
Northampton	8 55	11 45	4 50		7 25		
Weedon	9 1	12	2 44	4 49	8 17		4 20
Welton	9 22	1 16	5 10		8 23		4 50
London (Eustn.)	10 45	2 45	7 10		10 15		7 50
Birmingham	9 40	4 20	6 40		9 35		5 6
Manchester	12 30	4 20	8 20		9 53		5 37
Liverpool	12 40	4 40	8 40		11*37		5 45

THURSDAYS ONLY.

* Calls at Farthinghoe to pick up only. ‡ Calls at Farthinghoe to set down only.

Banbury station forecourt in 1950, block letters of London Midland & Scottish Railway evident. The tall metal chimney protruding above the roof on the right is from a raised hearth inside a small lean-to building. Construction of this building appears to be of early date but peculiarly there is no other entrance save the one inside the train shed, through a sliding wooden door. The hearth does not seem to have served any purpose in L.M.S. days, when salt was stored in the building. The strongest theory of its original use is that it was used to heat the cinders for the L.N.W.R. footwarmers in pre-train heat days.

L. & G.R.P.

superior ore through the port of Bilbao and the Welsh furnace owners turned their eyes away from the land and toward the incoming sea. A line across the Cotswolds was eventually built by the East and West Junction Railway.

Thenceforward the N&B lived a parlous existence running between the two towns of Northampton and Banbury with most rolling stock and locomotives hired from the LNWR. One of the locos that worked the line was a 'Sharpie' 2-2-2 converted into a saddle tank. By 1872 there were three regular passenger trains each way daily, which several years later were reduced to two. Locomotives purchased by the N&B from the LNWR were:

No. 1827	0-6-0	Built 1855
No. 1831	0-4-2T	Built 1852
No. 1849	0-6-0	Built 1849

The transactions for these locomotives were completed in 1872/3.

Early photographs of the appearance of Banbury (Merton Street) in the nineteenth century have been impossible to find. After the unfulfilled connection with the Oxford and Birmingham the LNWR seemed to have given it little attention, showing much greater interest in the cross-country line from Oxford to Cambridge which is not really surprising. One thing is certain and that is that the station layout and buildings at Banbury were kept as frugal as possible. The booking hall and offices at the front of the building are believed to be those of the original, together with the screens of the train shed. It is interesting to note that the platform was extended in three stages, the first was built as far as the side screens, this was of lateral wooden planking running from edge to edge. A few years later the more durable section built up from Staffordshire Blue pavoirs was installed, this would facilitate the early transportation of livestock before the cattle docks were built; a glance at the OS map of 1900 shows it in this condition. On the 1922 map the longitudinal timbers had taken the platform to its final length of 150 yards, shortening the carriage and van storage road at the platform end. The roof of the train shed was believed to have been built originally with two long gable sections running above each trackbed but was replaced by a single span glass-framed bow string roof supported by steel columns inside the screens, this roof is the one familiar in all the photographs. The stables appear to have been built some time between 1882 and 1898. The timber goods shed was built by the Buckinghamshire Railway shortly after the line's opening and in its original state contained two 30cwt. cranes; later another 5 ton crane was added outside in the yard. On the operating side it seems that the commodious locomotive shed was of similar vintage, it had the unrealised potential of storing eight locos, hardly the structure for the end of a minor branch. From its inception up to 1934 men were rostered from there as a sub-depot of Bletchley, although probably never more than a maximum of four 'sets' of men were employed.

Official Drawings of Banbury Goods Shed

Buckinghamshire Railway
Banbury Station
Goods Shed No 7

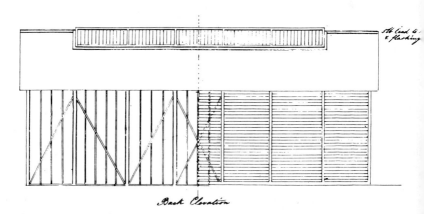

Sh lead to
& flashing

Back Elevation

Note. The Post &c to be placed
exactly in the centre
A Post under each of the Purlins
4½ × 6½

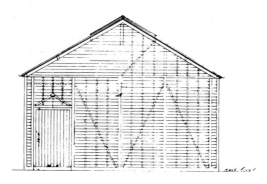

End Elevation

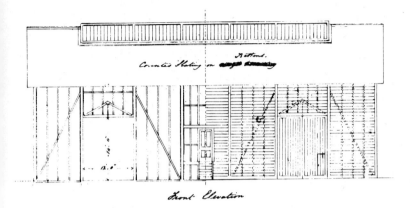

Front Elevation

The dotted lines at
T T &c show the position
of the Trusses to Roof

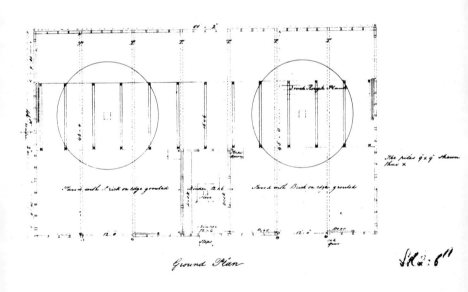

Ground Plan

Copy of original drawings for Banbury Goods shed dated 20th November, 1849
and from information received there was no alteration from these drawings to the
final structure.

A photograph taken just after the first world war, not a very clear print. The use of the gas lamp beside the carriage and van storage road on the right is interesting; it would often glow through the dark winter mornings when planks would be laid across the tracks and drays would move alongside this road to receive a load of milk.

Railway Magazine

Locomotives known to be in use on the branch in the early days were some of the 2-2-2 'Small Bloomers' with 6ft 6in driving wheel, later, up to 1906 a number of the 'Lady of the Lake' or 'Problem' class with 7ft 6in single driving wheel saw a great deal of service over the Buckinghamshire system together with some of the effete 2-4-0 6ft coupled 'Samson' class.

This would seem an appropriate point to introduce the works of Mr A.E. Grigg who has spent his life as a driver on the Buckinghamshire system together with his excellent work as an NUR official and author of a highly readable account of the history of the men of the Bletchley depot. Mr Grigg's book, 'In Railway Service', is a valuable contribution to the witness of courage and fortitude of railwaymen, one account concerning the 'Ladies' reads thus: 'The Ladies were adept at fast running and to the thrill, consternation or alarm — however one viewed it, — of the local residents and travellers, their drivers applied the same principles of gaining lost time to the Oxford locals as on a main-line. Compared with the main line expresses these locals were mere feather weights and when one of the Bletchley drivers decided to 'run' all conceptions of a Victorian branch line vanished. Trains of four or five six-wheeled coaches, weighing less than fifteen tons apiece, used to be hurtled up to 65, 70 and even 75 m.p.h. and there was one driver in particular who seemed to delight in scaring his guard; as the little high-flyer got into her stride, it is said that the white-bearded old patriarch at the rear end used to seize the hand brake in his van and screw it down hard to try to check their hurricane flight''.

Another and rather unusual visitor was the Webb compound tank No. 1967, that had somehow wandered beyond the London suburbs where it had spent its brief life. Much later in 1919 two 'Precedent' class or 'Jumbos' No's. 1168 'Cuckoo' and 193 'Rocket' ran regular turns up to Banbury. The real characteristic motive power of the branch for over sixty years were the ever popular Webb 2-4-2 Tank; 5ft 6 inches engines and the 18 inch 0-6-0 fast goods, (Cauliflowers) although numerous designs were seen on the branch these two stand out in their popularity and longevity.

As I have already mentioned the engine shed at Banbury was capable of storing eight locomotives maximum; it is probable that it never saw more than four in its long life time, except for very exceptional circumstances. The shed was of timber construction with a heavy slated roof supported with solid oak beams, the walls were heavily coated in pitch. The best tribute to its construction is that when the shed was closed, that is to say when it ceased to operate as an independently staffed shed in 1934, beneath the thickly coated whitewashed interior the wood was nearly as perfect as when installed, good enough for the Superintendent at Bletchley to make household furniture from it! Engines in residence at Banbury were four of the favoured 18 inch 'Cauliflowers' up to 1925 when only one remained. Originally the small turntable near the end of the cattle dock was replaced by a larger 42 ft one brought from the main depot at Bletchley in 1917, this was installed more conveniently behind the shed. Bill King the blacksmith at Bletchley maintained this table, he also maintained the water supply for the tank which was pumped from a spring near Farthinghoe station flowing downhill for four miles, along its course it also supplied the crossing house at Warkworth Crossing. The building upon which the tank rested was quite a high brick structure and served also as a three room dwelling house up to the first world war, for the 'driver in charge' Mr Plackett. During the first world war there were three 'sets' of men (a 'set' being a driver and fireman), who did all their own labouring with one of the drivers being in charge. From 1924 there was only one 'set' who booked on regularly at 1.30 pm to light up their own engine and shunt the goods yard then work a freight train to Brackley at 6.0 pm. At Brackley the method was to change engines with the down passenger train to Banbury, this saved the coaling of the Bletchley engine at Banbury. Originally this exchange was carried out at Buckingham. Once returned to Banbury the shunting would continue until the end of the shift when they would drop the fire and return home.

Recalling these days one of the footplatemen Arthur Grigg writes. . . "Arthur Elson was not too happy when transferred to Banbury in 1925 to cover the fireman's position there. It was a local agreement that Special Link firemen at Bletchley covered the out station depot vacancies and Arthur, despite repeated efforts was unable to return until 1934. On a permanent afternoon shift he fired his little 18 in. LNW

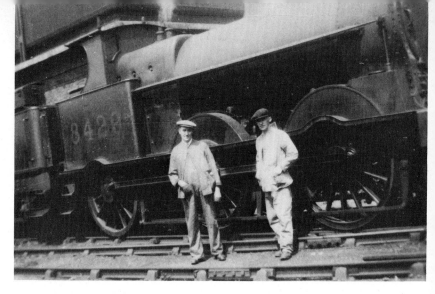

Albert Woodward (Driver) and Joe Jones (Fireman) pose for a photograph taken by one of the clerks in the Booking Office at Banbury as they pause in their day's duties at that station, in 1933. The engine is an 18" 0—6—0 Goods or 'Cauliflower'.

Albert Woodward

tender engine between Banbury and Buckingham. With driver Woodward they chugged along the country line in rain, snow or sunshine but the little narrow roof let in the weather, inclement or otherwise."

The depot became rather run down in the later years when the turntable became badly out of balance. After nationalisation loco's that required turning were authorised to go over to the Western Region for this facility, although some of the Bletchley men seemed to consider the small Merton Street table to be something of a challenge. One of these was a fireman called Cyril Gibbins who worked the branch in the early fifties and he assures me that rather than bow to the 'old enemy' he would turn his 'Super D' 0-8-0 thereon by screwing down the tender brakes and shunting the loco into the slack, the tolerance must have been inches! The shed itself was pulled down in the early 1930's but the water tank survived until 1960.

Little is known about the original signal box, up to 1930 it was probably an LNWR type 5 with the Webb lever frame. In that year it was altered rather curiously to a hybrid design with an LMS frame and a 'Midland' pattern cabin. The brick base retained LNWR characteristics. A very likely reason for the alteration could be the inclusion of outside ground frames, facilitating greater efficiency when dealing with the intensive cattle traffic at that time.

The electric train staff was brought into use on the branch on 14th September, 1890 two years after the station at Banbury had by an Act of Parliament been included within an extension of the Oxfordshire border into Northamptonshire.

Cheney's Railway Guide in 1916. The yearly guide continued until 1923 wh
serious fire at their printing works destroyed all of the type which was
irreplaceable.

Cheney &

30

Banbury and London (Euston).—L. & N. W. R.

STATIONS.		WEEK DAYS.																	SUND'YS

(Upward table — stations listed: BANBURY, Farthinghoe, Brackley, Fulwell, Buckingham, Padbury, Verney Jn., Quſⁿin. Rd., Aylesbury, Swanbourne, Winslow, Bletchley, Leighton, Dunstable, Luton, Cheddington, Tring, Berkhamsted, Watford, St. Albans, Willesden, Euston)

† Thursdays only.
‖ Saturdays only.

§ Thursdays excepted.
† Saturdays excepted.

(Downward table — stations: Euston, Willesden, St. Albans, Watford, Berkhamsted, Tring, Cheddington, Luton, Dunstable, Leighton, Bletchley, Winslow, Swanbourne, Aylesbury, Quſⁿin Rd., Verney Jn., Padbury, Buckingham, Fulwell, Brackley, Farthinghoe, BANBURY)

B Calls when required to pick up passengers.
a Saturdays 1.40

Banbury and Oxford.—L. & N. W. R. — Week Days only

STATIONS.	a.m.	a.m.		p.m.		p.m.	p.m.	p.m.		STATIONS.	a.m.	a.m.	a.m	noon	p.m.	p.m.	p.m.	p.m.	p.m.
BANBURY	7 40	9 35	…	…	…	…	2 30	4 55	7 30	Oxford M.	7 45	9 45	10 50	12 0	2 25	4 40	6 50	7 25
Verney Jn..dp	8 50	11 52	…	2 32	…	…	4 43	7 22		Islip	7 57	9 57	…	12 10	2 37	4 51	7	7 37
Bicester M.	8 55	12 2	…	2 38	…	…	4 48	7 27	P	Bicester M.	8 10	9 43	…	12 18	2 50	5 2	7	7 49
Launton	9 2	12 9	…	2 45	…	…	4 55	7 34		Launton	8 14	10 14	…	12 27	2 55	5 7	…	7 54
Marsh Gibbon	9 7	12 13	…	2 50	…	…	5 0	7 39		Marsh Gibbon	8 19	10 19	…	12 32	5 0	5 12	…	7 59
Claydon	9 13	12 19	12 35	2 55	4 9	5	5 7	7 45	9 46	Claydon	8 27	10 27	…	12 38	3 8	5 19	…	8 6
Islip	9 35	12 40	1 12	3 20	4 27	5 30	8 10	10		Verney Jn..ar	8 34	10 34	11 0	12 42	8 11	5 22	…	…
										BANBURY	9 26	11 47	…	…	2 55	6 32	6 32	…

STATIONS.	WEEK DAYS.						SUN.	STATIONS.	WEEK DAYS					SUN.
	a.m.	a.m.	p.m.	p.m.	p.m.	p.m.	p.m.		a.m.	a.m.	a.m.	a.m.	p.m.	a.m.
BANBURY dep.	7 40	9 35	2 30	4 55	7 30	7 30	7 30	Yarmouth ..dep.	…					
Bletchley .... arr.	9 7	10 40	3 40	6 20	8 42	8 42	8 33	Lowestoft ,,	…					
Bletchley ....dep.	9 52	11 18	3 52	5 6	9* 2		9 25	Norwich ,,	…					8 45
Northampton ..arr.	10 21	11 43	4 22	6‖56	10†0	10 0	9	Harwich ,,						
								Ipswich ,,						10 33

45

Ordnance Survey 1900 — 25 inches to the mile. Note the short platform and position of turntable, with smaller wagon turntables in goods shed and cattle pen areas. On this survey the locomotive facilities at the Great Western station appear to be more frugal than those of the L.N.W.R. Britannia Works tramway crosses the canal and River Cherwell to reach their rail depot.

Ordnance Surv

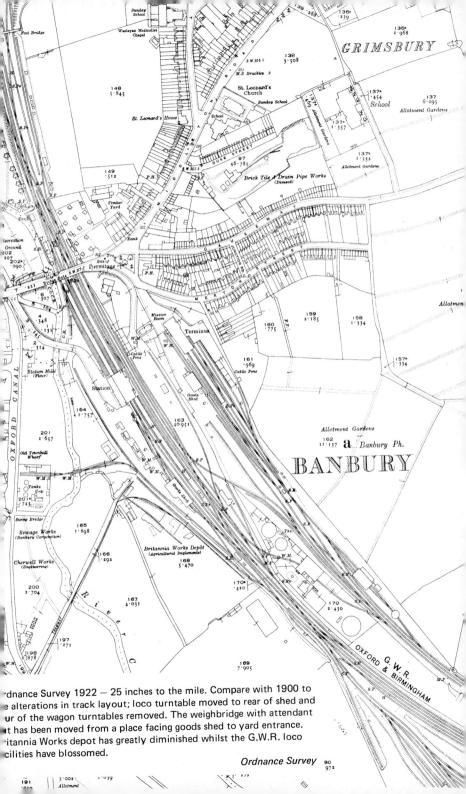

Ordnance Survey 1922 — 25 inches to the mile. Compare with 1900 to
the alterations in track layout; loco turntable moved to rear of shed and
four of the wagon turntables removed. The weighbridge with attendant
hut has been moved from a place facing goods shed to yard entrance.
Britannia Works depot has greatly diminished whilst the G.W.R. loco
facilities have blossomed.

Ordnance Survey

Mr E. Haslop, the penultimate Station Master at Banbury, circa 1905.

Mrs K. Greenland née Haslop

At the outbreak of the first World War Banbury (LNWR) was at its
zenith of passenger and goods traffic. The Northampton and Banbury
had been relieved of all its anxieties by having itself purchased by the
Stratford-upon-Avon and Midland Junction Railway in 1910 which
brought a number of through workings down that line; a local farming
family called Stroud used it almost like a personal transport. Staff at the
LNWR Station at that time included its longest serving Station Master
a Mr E.J. Haslop, who bred rabbits under the wooden platform.
Mr Haslop's staff included two booking clerks and twenty-six outside
men. Mr E.J. Haslop entered the Company's service at Cambridge in
1880; he then served as chief goods clerk at Rickmansworth, Leighton
Buzzard and Higham Ferrers, and came to Banbury in the same capacity
in 1892. In 1904 he was promoted to be Stationmaster and goods agent
from which position he retired in 1928. Mr Haslop with his wife and
eight children lived in a house nearby in Merton Street until his retirement when he went to live in No. 15, Calthorpe Road; it was from this
address that he was taken to an Oxford Hospital where he died in 1940.
Fortunately one of his daughters, Mrs M.K. Greenland, remembers those
early and very active days at the LNWR station very clearly. "The
station approach was always in first class order with its row of flowering
Lilac and Laburnum. The stables where four horses and their drays were
kept was also given the same care and attention by the two draymen,
Mr J. Bagley and Mr W. Lines, this area was always a great attraction for
youngsters. I remember how busy the goods department always seemed
to be and the impressive goods train with its cargo of monster Elms to
be delivered to A. Braggins, Timber Merchant.

My father's working day began when he left home at 7 o'clock for
his office, returning for breakfast at 8 o'clock. After returning he would
lunch from 1 to 2 and then work until tea at 5 o'clock, his final day's
duties would not cease until the departure of the last train, this was
usually at 8 o'clock. In winter he was often called out during the night
if snow had caused serious delays or accidents. Sundays were never really
free but he always attended church as a church warden.

His staff were always proud of the neat and clean appearance of the
station and waiting rooms, all of which were perfected by a delightful
display in the platform flowerbeds and rockery."

Interestingly, when Mr Haslop was succeeded by what became the
last stationmaster, Mr Horne, the position of goods agent became a
separate one, taken by Mr Haslop's son — Oliver Haslop.

Undoubtedly Mr Haslop would have been closely involved with part of
the large coal shipments that entered the town on both railways. One of
the earliest of these companies, W. Palmer and Son (c.1880) employed
their own wagons and rented storage space at the station for them.
Palmers also distributed from the other LNWR station at Farthinghoe. A
more recent colliery agent to be seen in the LMS yard was that of
B.T. Frost, who it is rumoured started their business as a result of the

frustratingly poor supplies during the general strike, they were founded about 1930. Hitherto they had only been concerned with the hay, straw and forage business. Arthur Elson who shunted at the station at that time said that 'Frost's wagons seemed to be everywhere'. The firm ceased trading independently and were absorbed by Charringtons in 1964.

During the period from 1901 to 1916 a through carriage from Euston was run being slipped at Bletchley in the down direction, and for a few

LICHFIELD T.V. TO LONDON (EUSTON) AND BRANCHES—continued.

ADDITIONAL RUNNING LINES.	STATIONS AND SIGNAL BOXES.			UP LINE.	Lie-by Sidings and holding capacity.		RUNAWAY CATCH POINTS.			ENGINE WHISTLES.					
	STATIONS AND SIGNAL BOXES, ETC.	Distance from place next above.			No. of Wagons.		WHERE SITUATE.	LINE.	Approximate Gradient.	UP.		DOWN.			
		Miles.	Yards.		Up Side.	Down Side.				Main, Fast or Passenger Line.	Slow or Goods Line.	Main, Fast or Passenger Line.	Slow or Goods Line.	TO	
							BANBURY STATION TO VERNEY JUNCTION.								
	Banbury—Station ..	—	—		....	....	....	....		....	....	1 crow and 1	}	No. 1 bay and vice versa	
										....	....	1 crow and 1	}	No. 2 ,, ,, ,,	
										2crows	....	and 2	}	Bays to turn table and vice versa ..	
										1 and	....	1 and	}		
										1 crow	....	1 crow	}	Sidings and vice versa	
	Farthinghoe—Station ..	3	1310		....	....	Between Banbury and Verney Junction	....		....	....	....	....	....	
	Cockley Brake Jn.	1	1042		....	....	....	....		1 5 short	....	1 3 short	....	Through .... Branch and vice versa	
	Brackley—Station ..	4	171		....	....	....	....		....	....	....	....		
	Fulwell & Westbury—†Station (Level Crossing)	2	1500		....	....	....	....		....	....	....	....		
	Buckingham—Station ..	4	779		....	88	....	....		....	....	....	....		
	Padbury—†Station ..	2	266		....	....	....	....		....	....	....	....		
	Verney Junction—Station .. See page 74.	2	596		....	....	....	.		....	....	....	....		

Details from Working Appendix, 1937.

C. Gibbins Collection

WORKING OF ROAD VANS.

No. of Road Van.	Labelled TO	Trains worked by			Stations served.	Remark
		Time of Departure	From	To		

The days on which the Vans leave the Starting Point are shown in the Remarks column.

From Banbury

8	Northampton ..	7 10 p.m.	Banbury ...	Blisworth ...	Helmdon, Wappenham,	Daily.
		12 30 a.m.	Blisworth ..	Northampton	Towcester, Northampton	
8a	Bletchley ...	4 45 p.m.	Banbury ...	Bletchley ..	Farthinghoe, Brackley.	Daily.
					Fulwell&W., Buckingham,	
					Padbury, Verney Junction,	
					Winslow, Swanbourne	

Pipe-fitted vehicle to be used. To be used as a Collecting Van only.

Working of Road Vans — Working time-table 1922.

J. Lowe

years after grouping in 1923 was restored, though at first the down train ran only as far as Buckingham. Amongst the numerous cattle trains for Banbury market were the horse boxes that ran to and from Newmarket, their owner's name emblazoned on the side. The goods trains of this pre-war period were often in the charge of an 0-6-0 DX class loco.

This was the life at Banbury when Europe stumbled into its first great catastrophe, the first world war, and Britain was to discover within the first twelve months what a terrible course that war would take, ruled by the big gun. In this event the only way towards any kind of solution would have to be in the engineering and ammunition factories of Britain, the house of Krupp would have to be matched shell for shell.

Early in 1916 the Ministry for Munitions occupied a farmland site about a mile and a half from the platform end at Banbury on the northern side of the branch near Warkworth Crossing. On this land they built a large shell filling factory with an extensive standard gauge railway system connected to the branch. Details concerning this factory are part of the work of a Banbury Historian Mr G.C.J. Hartland who has written many lucid accounts of the town's industrial history and to whom I am indebted for this and much more valuable information. He writes: "Extensive remains of the factory still exist and many of the old buildings and blast walls can still be identified. The factory was served by a standard gauge railway system that was served by a single line from a junction with the old LNWR, approximately three and a half miles of railway track existed on the site and the line of most of the old trackway is easily discernible today. The factory buildings comprised of concrete and wooden structures, some of them were surrounded by large earthworks. The filling houses were of wooden construction and were manned by four workers, two men and two women. Each shed was connected by two foot gauge tramways on which wooden trolleys were propelled by hand, carrying the various types of ammunition from stage to stage of their construction. All types of shell were dealt with at this factory, including H.E. gas and some types of mine. Shells were filled with lyddite and also mustard gas, they also handled naval mines, mortar bombs, shrapnel shells and anti-aircraft shells.

A serious explosion occurred in the site in 1917, in a department known as the Can Wash house. Several workers were seriously injured.

The factory had its own locomotive, an 0-6-0 saddle tank with outside cylinders named *Lidban* and numbered 1770. This was a popular industrial design and was produced in large numbers including 0-4-0's by Avonside Engineering Co.; *Lidban* was eventually sold to Brymbo Steel Co. in North Wales on the cessation of hostilities and closing of the works in 1919. It had employed 2000 personnel, 500 of them being women. When the last of those long trundling sinister cargoes had passed into silence the site was purchased by Messrs Cohen of London

This photograph of a Hudswell, Clarke 0-6-0 'saddle' tank *John* on the Ministry of Munitions site at Banbury was acquired very late in the book's production and afforded very little time for any research into its history. The maker's plate carries the date 1909 and it almost certainly preceded the arrival of *Lidban*. The curious enlargement on the top of the chimney is the understandable addition of a spark arrester, note also the electric lamp above the smokebox door.

Courtesy the late Mr. G. Insall

Arenig (formerly *Lidban*) belonging to Ministry of Munitions at their Banbury shell-filling factory. When the factory closed in 1919 the locomotive was sold to, and renamed by, the Brymbo Steel Co. Ltd., where she arrived on the 7th March in that year. The photograph shows her in service there on 24th April, 1949. She was replaced by a diesel locomotive in 1958 and subsequently scrapped on the spot. Details are as follows: Avonside Engineering Co. No. 1770 supplied new 1917. 0—6—0 outside cylinders (14" x 20") saddle tank, driving wheels 3'3".

T.J. Edgington

R.A.F. photograph taken on the 21 September 1954 clearly shows the layout of lines of the Ministry of Munitions factory near Banbury (top of page). The line turning from right converging with the branch before Banbury is the Oxford—Birmingham of the G.W.R.

Interesting to note that the roof of the ex L.M.S. station was removed two years before the railcar experiment and not immediately preceding it. Nostalgic wiffs of steam curl up from the ex G.W.R. depot bottom right. The gasworks is still in its complete form, the open rectangle between this structure and the twisting river Cherwell is the still extant, Banbury United football ground.

Department of the Environment

Government Munitions Siding, Banbury.—The points leading from the single line to Munition Siding are controlled by the electric train staff.

A ballast train, goods train, or L. & N. W. engine may be required to work in the Siding Banbury Munitions Factory or Farthinghoe Station, and afterwards return to Banbury proceed to Cockley Brake Junction.

After the engine or the engine and the whole train has run clear into the Munitions Sid the guard or shunter in charge will be responsible for seeing that the Main Line is clear.

Drivers are authorised to hand the staff to the guard or shunter, who, after the trai engine is clear in the Siding, will return to Banbury Box and hand the signalman the staff.

When work is completed and the train or engine is ready to leave the Munitions Siding return to Banbury or proceed to Cockley Brake Junction as may be required, the guard or shu will proceed to Banbury Box, and a staff will be handed to the guard or shunter to give to driver.

An engine after disposing of its train in the Munitions Siding is authorised to return ligh Banbury. (10/1

Special instructions for Government Munitions siding, Banbury.

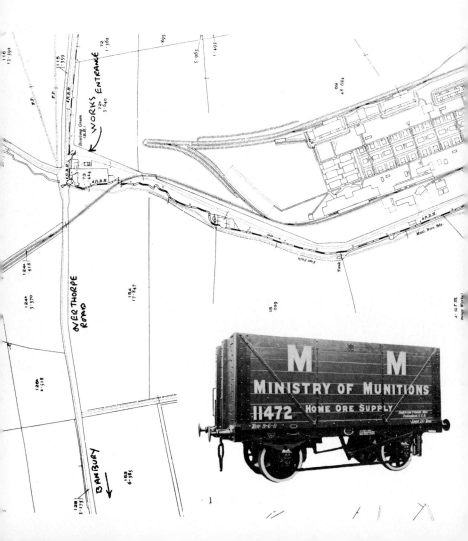

Layout of tracks and buildings in the Ministry of Munitions ammunition factory at Banbury. The junction to the branch can be seen below, the small house nearby is at Warkworth Crossing that carries the footpath from Bodicote to Warkworth across the line and over the Ministry of Defence lines. The track leading off at the top of the page crosses the Overthorpe Road through unmanned gates and then splits into two prongs in the fields diverting away from each other with a wooden store building at the end of each.

1922 Ordnance Survey

to be used as a breaking-down factory. Breaking-down is the process of destroying thousands of tons of war materials and this continued until 1924, during that period there had been five fatal accidents emphasising the greater danger of dismantling the ageing material.

One of the delightful people that I have met whilst working on this history is Mrs Neville, daughter of Mrs Butcher who was responsible for the control of 'Butcher's' Crossing or Warkworth Crossing and had been so employed there by the LNWR from 1903, until the crossing became unmanned in 1942. Mrs Butcher must have witnessed the period of the line's most intense activity and in payment for her services she received ten shillings and sixpence (52½p) per week plus one free train ride a year, one other at half fare and three passes at a third of the price for relatives. (Not to mention the unofficial requirement of challenging a runaway bullock for which she contracted a broken shoulder.) Mrs Neville remembered quite clearly her childhood in the lonely crossing keeper's house and the period of the breaking-down factory when the air was rent with terrible explosions — reverberations of the Somme in Oxfordshire. When the breaking-down was finished the site was given up to the rabbits and pheasants, and grass. This lasted until the second world war when the site was enlisted once more, this time as a bombing range by both the regular army and Home Guard. The 4th/7th Dragoon Guards who were stationed in Banbury during this war left an old Covenenter tank on the site that they had used for target practice until its battered and rusty remains were dragged away for scrap. In 1940 a lone Heinkel dropped five bombs on the site, possibly the Germans believed that it was still serving its first war purpose. At the end of that war it became an area to graze cattle, as it is today.

Returning to the early period of the 1920's one sees the station passing out of its prime although Banbury industry was still developing. After the rush of converging troop trains the passenger traffic at the LNWR began to drift more so to the Great Western station which was by now becoming the principal railhead of the town, although the old Buckinghamshire line was still carrying a fair burden of the cattle and freight requirements.

In 1920 United Dairies made Banbury a collecting centre for their milk which was certainly beneficial to the railways. On March 28th, 1929 this company announced the early use of glass-lined tanks carrying milk in bulk from the LMS and GWR at Banbury. So successful were they that they also began to work north on the ex-GC line of the LNER later that year. A most important development as far as the branch was concerned was the purchase of a site alongside the station for the Midland Marts Company stockyard, to load and unload the cattle into a market complex which they controlled. This took place in 1921 and I think there is little doubt that this single and highly significant development put many years on the branch's life. The cattle pens

Mrs. Butcher stands outside her crossing keepers house at Warkworth (Butcher's) Crossing. The footpath to Warkworth across the trackbed is still used but there is not the slightest trace of the house and garden.

Mrs Neville née Butcher

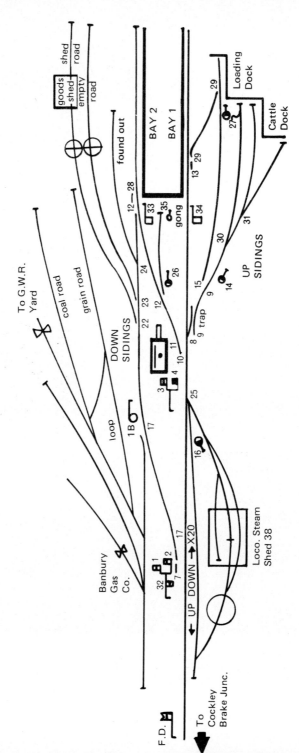

BANBURY
L. & N.W. Rly.

To G.W.R. Yard

goods shed road
goods shed empty road

found out

BAY 2
BAY 1

Loading Dock

Cattle Dock

coal road

grain road

DOWN SIDINGS

loop

1B

17

gong

UP SIDINGS

33
35
34
13 29
29
27
26
24
23
12
15
14
9
8 9 trap
10
11
4
3
25
31
30

Banbury Gas Co.

32
1
2
7

UP DOWN → X20

17

UP
DOWN

To Cockley Brake Junc.

Loco. Steam Shed 38

F.D.

16

58

SPARE 5, 6, 19 & 21.

Diagram showing lever numbers for points and signals at Banbury.

were extended to the length apparent on the 1922 map and were prepared to be intensely active. Much of the traffic was now goods, ore and livestock. In all there were eight cattle pens with accommodation for loading and unloading thirteen cattle trucks at once, with siding accommodation for thirty-four more. A driver, Mr Sharp, booked one train of forty cattle vans to be taken to Cambridge. There were also facilities for dealing with horses and carriages and sufficient sidings for two hundred and seventeen mixed wagons. The company did all its own carting and had stable accommodation for its nine horses. So it was in this moderately prosperous existence that the branch faced the national grouping of the largest and smallest of railway companies into the 'big four', and the line passed out of the ownership of the LNWR who had controlled it for over seventy years, into the organization of the London, Midland and Scottish Railway Company. During this company's ownership the addition of 'Merton Street' appeared on the station signs.

The new company did not alter the locomotive types on the branch very much save for the occasional rambling Midland 0-6-0 4F which became a more common engine in the 1940's and 1950's, but they did remove the locomotive shed in the early thirties leaving of course the tank house and turntable, thenceforth all engine diagrams operated from Bletchley.

Another incident to affect the town and railway cartage in the depressed thirties was the fall of Samuelsons, luckily for Banbury the effects upon employment were somewhat mitigated by the arrival of the Northern Aluminium Co. (later Alcan) from West Bromwich in 1931. For the LMS it was more of a loss than a gain as most of the new company's requirements would be ably filled by the GWR as the latter company's complex had become quite widespread with a large locomotive depot.

Each day small goods were allocated to a Bletchley van and a Northampton van, the latter having the nickname 'The Dilly' which I am told is something to do with a small pig, a vague association which was ascribed in some way to its junior requirements. In 1936 the LMS were eager to dispense with small parcel traffic and concentrate on only the larger requirements of goods. To this effect they approached the GWR with a pooling arrangement whereby all small goods in Banbury would be handled by them and any loaded vans would be shunted across the exchange siding to be accepted by an LMS loco. The Great Western agreed and relieved the LMS of their burden. It is amusing to recollect that in the days of the 'Premier Line' the staff at Merton Street would rather send a single parcel destined for Oxford, via Verney Junction, than hand it over to the 'old enemy'.

On this agreement the LMS decided to demolish the huge and ageing timber goods shed and replace it with a red brick utilitarian structure that conceded nothing to taste; ironically that eyesore is the

Distance from Bletchley.	Distance from Bletchley.	WEEK DAYS.	1	2	3	4	5	6	7	8	9	10	11	12
				Mineral.	Goods.	Light Engine.	Mail & Goods.	Mail & Goods.	Motor.	Goods.	Pass.	Pass.	S. M. J. Pass.	
				M	MO	M								
Miles	Miles.			a.m.	a.m	a.m.	a.m.	a.m.	a.m.	a.m.	a.m.	a.m.	a.m.	
...	...	BLETCHLEY JUNC. dep.	...	2 0	2 0	4 0	4 20	...	...	6 20	8 15	8 35	...	...
5¼	5¼	Swanbourne ... ... ,,	...	...	...	...	...	...	...	7 0	8 26	8 46	...	...
7¼	7¼	Winslow ... ... arr.	...	...	...	4 15	4 38	...	...	7 15	8 30	8 50	...	...
		Winslow dep.	...	...	...		4 53	...	...	8 5	8 32	8 53	...	...
9½	9½	Verney Junc. ... arr.	...	...	2 50	...	4 58	...	...		8 37	8 58	...	...
		Verney Junc. dep.	...	2 40	...	...	5 21	5 8	...	Swanbourne arr. 6.45 Claydon arr. 8.20	8 40	9 1	...	...
11⅞	...	Padbury ... ... ,,	...	...	...	...	...	...	...		8 48	...	...	...
14	...	Buckingham ... arr.	...	8 45 p.m. from Nuneaton	...	...	5 31	...	...		8 54	...	...	...
		Buckingham dep.	...		...	...	5 33	...	...		8 57	...	...	...
18⅜	...	Fulwell & Westbury ,,	...		...	...	...	...	...		9 7	...	...	...
21¼	...	Brackley ... ... arr.	...		...	...	5 49	...	...		9 14	...	...	...
		Brackley dep.	...		...	...	5 51	...	...		9 28	...	...	...
25⅝	...	Cockley Brake Junc. ,,	...		...	...	6§0	...	...		9§37	...	9 55	...
26⅞	...	Farthinghoe ... ... ,,	...		...	...	...	...	...		9 41	...	9 59	...
30⅞	...	BANBURY ... ... arr.	...	...	...	...	6 15	...	...		9 50	...	10 8	...
...	11¼	Claydon ... ... dep.	...	...	...	...	...	...	...	8 35	...	9 6	...	...
...	...	Itter's Brick Siding ... ,,	...	...	...	...	...	...	...	...	...	...	...	...
...	15⅛	Marsh Gibbon & Pound'n ,,	...	...	...	...	...	...	...	...	...	9 17	...	...
...	17¼	Launton ... ... ,,	...	...	...	...	...	...	...	...	...	9 23	...	...
...	19½	Bicester ... ... arr.	...	...	...	...	...	5 26	...	9 0	...	9 28	...	...
		Bicester dep.	...	...	...	...	...	5 28	8 15	9 10	...	9 31	...	...
...	20¾	Wendlebury ... ... ,,	...	...	...	...	...	...	8 19	...	...	...	...	...
...	22⅞	Charlton ... ... ,,	...	...	...	...	...	...	8 25	...	...	...	...	...
...	24⅛	Oddington ... ... ,,	...	...	...	...	...	...	8 29	...	...	...	...	...
...	25½	Islip ... ... ,,	...	...	...	...	...	...	8 33	X	...	9 43	...	...
...	27¾	Oxford Road ... arr.	...	3 40	...	...	...	...	...	9 30	...	...	...	...
		Oxford Road dep.	...	4 0	...	...	...	...	8 39	9 55	...	...	...	...
...	29	Wolvercote ... ... ,,	...	...	...	...	...	...	8 42	...	...	...	...	...
...	30⅜	Port Meadow ... ... ,,	...	...	...	...	...	...	8 45	...	...	...	...	...
...	31⅜	OXFORD ... ... arr.	...	4 15	...	...	...	5 52	8 48	10 5	...	9 55	...	...

WEEK DAYS—*Continued.*	13	14	15	16	17	18	19	20	21	22	23	24	25	26	27
	Motor.	Pass.	Pass.	Pass.	Mineral.	Goods.	Pass.	Pass.	Motor.	Pass.	Motor.	Pass.	Light Engine.	Mineral.	
			TH O												
	a.m.	a.m.	a.m.	a.m.	a.m.	a.m.	a.m.	p.m.	p.m.	p.m.	p.m.	p.m.	p.m.	p.m.	
BLETCHLEY J. dep.	...	10 10	...	Thursdays excepted.	10 15	11 0	11 50	12 10	12 20	1†25	...	1 40	...	1 45	...
Swanbourne ... ,,	...	10 21	...		...	...	...	12 21	12 32	1 36	...	1 50	...	...	...
Winslow ... arr.	...	10 25	...		10 45	11 30	...	12 25	12 37	1 40	...	1 54	...	2 15	...
Winslow dep.	...	10 29	...		11 0	11 45	...	12 28	12 40	1 42	...	2 1		2 20	...
Verney Junc. arr.	...	10 34	...		11 10	11 55		12 33	12 45	1 47	...	2 6	...	2 30	...
Verney Junc. dep.	...	10 39	10 45	10 45	11 20	12 10	...	12 38	12 49	1 48	...	2 8	...	2 45	...
Padbury ... ,,	...	...	10 51	10 51	11 35	...	9.45 a.m. from Cambridge.	...	12 57	...	...	2 16	...	Arr. Itter's Sdg. 2.55, Islip 4.20	...
Buckingham arr.	...	...	10 57	10 57	11 45	...		...	1 5	...	...	2 21	...		...
Buckingham dep.	...	...	11 2	11 2	1 40	12§30		...		† Public Bills 1.20 p.m.	...	2 25	...		...
Fulwell & W. ,,	...	...	11 13	11 13	2 0	...		...	...		...	2 35	...		...
Brackley... arr.	...	...	11 20	11 20	2 10	12 50		...	...		...	2 41	...		...
Brackley dep.	...	...	11 28			1 0		...	...		...	2 46	...		...
Cockley Brake J. ,,	...	...	11§38	...	...	1§10		...	...	...	...	2§55	...		...
Farthinghoe ... ,,	...	...	11 43	...	...	1 25		...	...	...	...	2 59	...		...
BANBURY .. arr.	...	...	11 52	...	...	1 45	...	...	...	...	...	3 8	...		...
Claydon ... ...dep.	...	10 44	...	...	...	...	...	12 43	...	1 53	...	...	...	...	...
Itter's Brick Sdg. ,,	...	...	...	...	...	...	...	...	...	...	...	...	...	3 10	...
Marsh Gibbon & P. ,,	...	10 53	...	...	...	Farthinghoe arr. 1.15 p.m.	...	12 52	...	2 2	...	...	...	...	...
Launton ... ,,	...	10 58	...	...	...		...	12 58	...	2 7	...	...	...	...	...
Bicester ... arr.	...	11 3	...	...	...		12 15	1 3	...	2 12		Padbury arr. 2.13 p.m.	...	3 35	...
Bicester dep.	10 20	11 5	...	...	...		12 17	1 5	...	2 13	2 30		...	4 5	...
Wendlebury ... ,,	10 25	...	...	...	...		...	...	...	...	2 35		...	...	...
Charlton ... ,,	10 31	...	...	...	...		...	...	...	...	2 41		...	...	...
Oddington .. ,,	10 36	...	...	...	...	...	...	...	...		2 46		...	...	...
Islip ... ... ,,	10 40	11 17	...	...	...	...	...	1 17	...	2 25	2 50		...	4 35	...
Oxford Road arr.	...	...	...	...	...	...	...	...	...	...	...		...	4 45	...
Oxford Road dep.	10 47	...	...	...	...	...	...	...	...	...	2 57	...	4 30	5 15	...
Wolvercote ... ,,	10 51	...	...	...	...	...	...	...	...	...	3 1	...	...	...	...
Port Meadow ... ,,	10 54	...	...	...	...	...	...	...	...	...	3 4	...	...	...	...
OXFORD ... ...arr.	10 57	11 29	...	...	...	...	12 33	1 29	...	2 38	3 7	...	4 38	5 25	...

Single Line, Verney Junction to Banbury.—Electric Train Staff Stations—Verney Junction, Buckingham, Brackley, Cockley Brake Junction, and Banbury.
Passenger Trains can cross each other at Buckingham, Brackley, and Cockley Brake Junction only.

Working time-table 1922. Note the L.N.W.R. steam rail motor is enjoying a revival, trying to combat the incursion of omnibuses.

John Lowe

WEEK DAYS—Continued.	28	29	30	31	32	33	34	35	36	37	38	39	40
		S. M. J. Goods.	Motor.	Pass.		Motor.	Motor.	S. M. J. Pass.	Pass.	Pass.	Pass.	Empty Coaches. SO	Goods. S
		p.m.	p.m.	p.m.		p.m.	p.m.	p.m.	p.m.	p.m.	p.m.	p.m.	p.m.
BLETCHLEY J. dep.	...	...	4† 5	4 30	...	4 45	...	...	5 25	7 0	7 12	...	11 30
Swanbourne ... ,,	...	...	4 16	4 41	...	4 56	...	...	5 36	7 11	7 25	...	...
Winslow ... arr.	...	...	4 20	4 45	...	5 0	...	...	5 40	7 15	7 29	...	...
Winslow ... dep.	...	...		4 50	...	5 5	...	...	5 43	7 17	7 33	...	...
Verney Junc. arr.	...	...	...	4 55	...	5 10	...	...	5 48	7 22	7 38	...	12 20
Verney Junc. dep.	...	...	...	4 58	...	5 11	...	...	5 53	7 23	7 39	...	...
Padbury ... ... ,,	...	...	† Public Bills 4.0 p.m.	...	...	5 17	...	...	5 59	7 29	...	...	...
Buckingham arr.	...	...		...	...	5 22	...	...	6 4	7 34	...	...	...
Buckingham dep.	...	...		...	...	5 27	...	...	6 6	7 39	...	...	...
Fulwell & W. ,,	...	...		...	...	5 37	...	...	6 16	7 49	...	...	...
Brackley arr.	...	...		...	...	5 43	...	...	6 22	7 55	...	...	...
Brackley dep.	...	...		...	...	5 44	...	...		7 59	...	...	...
Cockley Brake J. ,,	...	3§50		...	...	5§53	...	6§12	...	8§ 8	...	...	...
Farthinghoe ... ,,	...	4 0	...	...	...	5 57	...	6 17	...	8 12	...	...	...
BANBURY ... arr.	...	4 10	...	...	...	6 5	...	6 25	...	8 20	...	...	...
Claydon ... ... dep.	...	...	...	5 3	...	...	...	...	...	...	7 45	...	...
Itter's Brick Sdg. ,,	...	...	...	...	...	...	...	...	...	...	...	...	...
Marsh Gibbon & P. ,,	...	...	...	5 13	...	...	...	...	...	...	7 56	...	...
Launton ... ... ,,	...	...	...	5 19	...	...	...	...	...	...	8 2	...	...
Bicester ... arr.	...	...	...	5 24	...	...	...	...	...	...	8 7	...	...
Bicester ... dep.	...	...	...	5 26	...	...	6 5	...	...	...	8 11	9 50	...
Wendlebury ... ,,	...	...	...	...	...	...	6 10	...	...	...	...	...	...
Charlton ... ... ,,	...	...	...	...	...	...	6 16	...	...	...	...	...	...
Oddington ... ... ,,	...	...	...	...	...	...	6 21	...	...	...	...	...	...
Islip ... ... ,,	...	...	...	5 38	...	...	6 25	...	...	...	8 25	...	...
Oxford Road arr.	...	...	...	...	...	...	...	...	...	...	...	...	...
Oxford Road dep.	...	...	...	...	...	...	6 32	...	...	...	...	...	...
Wolvercote ... ,,	...	...	...	...	...	...	6 36	...	...	...	...	...	...
Port Meadow ... ,,	...	...	...	...	...	...	6 39	...	...	...	...	...	...
OXFORD ... ... arr.	...	...	...	5 50	...	...	6 42	...	...	...	8 38	10 15	...

SUNDAYS.	1	2	3	4	5	6	7	8	9	10	11	12	13
		Goods.				Milk & Mails.	Milk.		Pass.		Pass.	Light Engine.	
		a.m.				a.m.	a.m.		p.m.		p.m.	p.m.	
BLETCHLEY J. dep.	...	2 0	...	...	...	6 0	...	...	1 20	...	...	6 0	...
Swanbourne ... ,,	...	...	...	...	...	6 15	...	...	1 39	...	...	...	...
Winslow ... arr.	...	2 35	...	...	...	6 20	...	...	1 37	...	...	...	...
Winslow ... dep.	...	2 45	...	...	...	6 22	...	...	1 42	...	...	...	...
Verney Junc. arr.	...	...	...	...	...	6 28	...	...	1 48	...	...	...	...
Verney Junc. dep.	...	...	...	...	...	6 30	7 40	...	1 58	...	4 45	6§20	...
Padbury ... ... ,,	...	...	...	...	...	6 37	...	...	...	...	4 51	...	...
Buckingham arr.	...	...	...	...	...	6 45	...	...	...	...	4 56	...	...
Buckingham dep.	...	...	...	...	...		...	...	...	...	4 59	6§31	...
Fulwell & W. ,,	...	...	...	...	...	...	...	...	...	...	5 9	...	...
Brackley ... arr.	...	...	...	...	...	...	...	...	...	...	5 15	...	...
Brackley ... dep.	...	...	...	...	...	...	...	...	...	...	5 18	6§47	...
Cockley Brake J. ,,	...	...	...	...	...	...	...	...	...	...	5§27	6§57	...
Farthinghoe ... ,,	...	...	...	...	...	...	...	...	...	...	...	...	...
BANBURY ... arr.	...	...	...	...	...	...	...	...	...	...	5 40	7 10	...
Claydon ... ... dep.	...	...	...	...	...	...	...	...	2 8	...	...	...	...
Marsh Gibbon & P. ,,	...	...	...	...	...	...	...	...	2 12	...	...	...	...
Launton ... ... ,,	...	...	...	...	...	...	...	...	2 18	...	...	...	...
Bicester ... arr.	...	...	...	...	...	...	8 0	...	2 23	...	...	...	...
Bicester ... dep.	...	...	...	...	...	...		...	2 25	...	...	...	...
Wendlebury ... ,,	...	...	...	...	...	...	...	...	...	...	...	...	...
Charlton ... ... ,,	...	...	...	...	...	...	...	...	...	...	...	...	...
Oddington ... ... ,,	...	...	...	...	...	...	...	...	...	...	...	...	...
Islip ... ... ,,	...	...	...	...	...	...	...	...	2 37	...	...	...	...
Oxford Road arr.	...	3 35	...	...	...	...	...	...	...	...	...	...	...
Oxford Road dep.	...	3 50	...	...	...	...	...	...	...	...	...	...	...
Wolvercote ... ,,	...	...	...	...	...	...	...	...	...	...	...	...	...
Port Meadow ... ,,	...	...	...	...	...	...	...	...	...	...	...	...	...
OXFORD ... ... arr.	...	4 5	...	...	...	...	...	...	2 50	...	...	...	...

Single Line, Verney Junction to Banbury.—Electric Train Staff Stations—Verney Junction, Buckingham, Brackley, Cockley Brake Junction, and Banbury.

NOTE.—The Crossing Gates at Fulwell & Westbury are put across the Line after the passage of the 7.15 p.m. Goods from Banbury each night until 6.0 a.m. next morning. On Sundays the Crossing Gates will only be opened for the passage of Passenger Trains. The Drivers of the 4.20 a.m. Goods from Bletchley, and of any Special Train that may require to run over the Branch during the hours the Gates are across the Line, must stop at the Gates so that the Guard may open them for the passage of the Train, and replace them after the Train has passed over the Crossing.

Distance from Oxford.	Distance from Banbury.	WEEK DAYS.		1 Goods.	2 Goods.	3 Goods.	4 Pass.	5 Motor.	6 Pass	7 Pass.	8 Pass.	9 Motor	10 S. M. J. Pass.	11 Pass.	12
Miles.	Miles.			a.m.	a.m.	a.m.	a.m.	a.m.	a.m.	a.m.	a.m.	a.m.	a.m.		
...	...	OXFORD	dep.	M	...	MO	7 15	7 30	...	...	9 15	9 35	...	a.m	...
1	...	Port Meadow	,,	...	...	...	...	7 33	...	...	...	9 38	...	...	...
2⅝	...	Wolvercote	,,	...	...	...	...	7 36	...	...	...	9 41	...	...	...
3½	...	Oxford Road ...	arr.	...	...	...	...	...	...	...	...	...	...	...	...
			dep.	...	...	...	...	7 40		...	...	9 45	...	...	...
5⅞	...	Islip	arr.	...	...	...	7 26	...	Farthinghoe arr. 7.33 a.m., Padbury arr. 8.17 a.m.	...	9 26	...	...	...	...
			dep.	...	...	...	7 29	7 47		...	9 28	9 52	...	...	...
7¼	...	Oddington	,,	...	...	...	...	7 51		...	...	9 56	...	...	...
8½	...	Charlton	,,	...	...	...	...	7 56		...	...	10 1	...	...	...
10⅝	...	Wendlebury..	,,	...	...	...	...	8 2		...	...	10 7	...	...	...
11⅞	...	Bicester	arr.	...	...	...	7 40	8 7		...	9 39	10 12	...	...	...
			dep.	...	,,	...	7 43			...	9 41		...	...	...
14⅛	...	Launton	arr.	...	...	...	7 48	...		...	...	...	...	...	...
			dep.	...	...	...	7 50	...		...	9 46	...	...	...	...
16¼	...	Marsh Gibbon & Poundon	,,	...	...	...	8 0	...		...	9 52	...	...	...	...
...	...	Itter's Brick Siding ...	,,	...	...	...	...	...		...	...	...	...	...	...
17¾	...	Charndon Bridge Milk Stage	arr.	...	...	...	8 4	...	...	...	...	...	...	...	...
			dep.	...	...	...	8 6	...	...	...	...	...	...	...	...
20⅛	...	Claydon	,,	...	...	...	8 13	...	...	...	10 1	...	...	...	...
...	...	BANBURY ...	dep	...	...	...		...	7 25	9 5	...	...	10 30		...
...	4	Farthinghoe	,,	...	...	...		...	7 36	9 14	...	...	10 39		...
...	5½	Cockley Brake Junc....	,,		...			...	7§40	9§18	...	...	10§43	Thurs. excepted	...
...	9⅝	Brackley	arr.	To Rugby.	...	To Hillmorton.	Arrive Marsh Gibbon 7.55, Swanbourne 8.31	...	7 48	9 26	...	...	...		...
			dep.		...			...	7 50	9 28	...	...	...	11 40	...
...	12½	Fulwell & Westbury	,,		...			...	7 57	9 35	...	...	...	11 47	...
...	16⅞	Buckingham ...	arr.		...			...	8 6	9 44	...	...	...	11 56	...
			dep.		...			...	8 12	9 47	...	...	...	11 57	...
...	19	Padbury	,,	...	...	...		...	8 21	9 53	...	...	...	12 3	...
21⅞	21⅜	Verney Junc. ...	arr.	...	...	...	8 17	...	8 26	9 58	10 5	...	...	12 8	...
			dep.	3 0	...	5 30	8 19	...	8 30	10 0	10 7	...	...	12 10	...
24⅛	23⅝	Winslow	arr.	3 10	...	5 40	8 24	...	8 35	10 5	10 12	...	...	12 15	...
			dep.	3 20	4 40	5 50	8 27	...	8 40	10 7	10 15	...	...		...
26⅛	25⅝	Swanbourne	,,	...	...	...	8 35	...	8 46	...	10 20	...	...	...	...
31⅝	30⅞	BLETCHLEY JUNC.	arr.	3 50	5 10	6 20	8 45	...	8 55	10 21	10 31	...	...	...	...

WEEK DAYS—*Continued.*		13 Goods.	14 Mineral	15 Pass.	16 Motor.	17 Motor.	18 Pass.	19 Pass.	20 Goods.	21 Light Engine.	22 Pass.	23 Motor.	24 Mixed.	25 Mixed.	26 Goods.	27
									SO				SO	S	WO	
		a.m.	a.m.	a.m.	p.m.	p.m.	p.m.	p.m.	p.m.	p.m.	p.m	p.m.	p.m.	p.m.	p.m.	
OXFORD ...	dep.	10 20	10 50	11 30	...	1 15	2 0	...	...	3 0	3 10	...	...	...	3 15	...
Port Meadow ...	,,	...	...	...	...	1 18	...	...		...	...	...	...	...	...	...
Wolvercote ...	,,	...	...	...	...	1 21	...	...	...	...	...	...	...	...	...	...
Oxford Road	arr.	...	11 0	...	...	...	...	...	...	3 8	...	...	...	...	...	...
	dep.	...	12 45	...	...	1 25	...	...	...		...	...	...	...	...	...
Islip	arr.	10 40	...	...	...	...	...	...	...	...	...	...	...	...	...	...
	dep.	11 5	...	11 42	...	1 32	2 12	...	...	...	...	...	...	...	...	...
Oddington .	,,	...	...	...	...	1 36	...	...	...	...	...	...	...	...	...	...
Charlton	,,	...	...	...	...	1 41	...	...	...	...	...	...	...	...	...	...
Wendlebury ...	,,	...	...	...	...	1 47	...	...	...	...	...	...	...	...	...	...
Bicester ...	arr.	11 20	...	11 53	...	1 52	2 23	...	...	...	3 28	...	...	...	3 50	...
	dep.	12 5	...	11 55	...		2 25	...	...	...	3 30	...	...	...	4 0	...
Launton ...	arr.	12 13	...	...	...	...	...	...	...	...	...	...	...	...	...	...
	dep.	12 30	...	12 1	...	...	2 31	...	...	...	...	...	...	...	...	...
Marsh Gibbon & P.	,,	1 0	...	12 7	...	...	2 37	...	...	...	...	...	...	...	...	...
Itter's Brick Sdg.	,,	...	...	...	...	...	...	...	...	...	...	...	...	...	...	...
Claydon	,,	1 30	...	12 16	...	...	2 46	...	...	...	...	...	...	...	...	...
BANBURY ...	dep.		...	...	...	...	...	2 20	...	...	...	...	...	...	...	...
Farthinghoe ...	,,		...	...	...	...	...	2 29	...	...	...	...	...	...	...	...
Cockley Brake J.	,,		...	...	...	...	...	2§35	...	...	...	...	...	...	...	...
Brackley ...	arr.	Marsh Gibbon arr. 12.40 p.m., Claydon arr. 1.10 p.m.	...	...	...	...	...	2 43	...	...	...	...	...	...	...	...
	dep.		...	...	...	...	...	2 46	3 20	...	...	...	...	3 55	...	...
Fulwell and W.	,,		...	...	...	...	...	2 53	...	...	...	...	...	4 3	...	...
Buckingham	arr.				...	...	...	3 2	3 40	...	...	...	...	4 17	...	...
	dep.		...	...	1 15	...	...	3 6		...	...	...	4 19	4 19	...	...
Padbury	,,		...	...	1 22	...	...	3 12	...	...	...	...	4 26	4 26	...	...
Verney Junc.	arr.	1 35	...	12 20	1 27	...	2 50	3 17	...	...	...	...	4 32	4 32	4 35	...
	dep.	1 45	...	12 22	1 29	...	2 52	3 19	...		...	...	4 35	4 35	4 45	...
Winslow ...	arr.	1 55	2 5	12 27	1 34	...	2 57	3 24	...	...	3 51	...	4 42	4 42	4 55	...
	dep	3 10	2 10	12 30	1 36	...	3 0	3 28	...	...	3 58	4 25	4 44	4 44	5 20	...
Swanbourne ...	,,	...	...	12 35	1 42	...	3 5	3 34	...	...	...	4 30	4 50	4 50	...	...
BLETCHLEY J.	arr.	3 35	2 45	12 46	1 53	...	3 22	3 45	...	...	4 12	4 41	5 5	5 5	5 45	...

Single Line, Banbury to Verney Junction.—Electric Train Staff Stations—Banbury, Cockley Brake Junction, Brackley, Buckingham, and Verney Junction.

WEEK DAYS.	28	29	30	31	32	33	34	35	36	37	38	39	40	41	42
	Goods.	Pass.	Pass.	S.M.J. Pass.	Motor.	Pass.	Motor.	Pass.	S.M.J. Goods.	Goods.	Goods.	Pass.	Fast Goods.	Fast Goods.	
	TH O p.m.	p.m.	p.m.	p.m.	p.m.	p.m.		p.m.	p.m.	p.m.	SO p.m.	SO p.m.	p.m.	p.m.	
OXFORD ... ...dep.	...	4 40	...	...	5 0			7 5	...	6 50	...	9 15	10 55	11 35	...
Port Meadow ... ,,	...	...	...	...	5 3			...	...	...	...	...	...	...	...
Wolvercote ... ,,	...	...	...	...	5 6		Buckingham	...	...	...	...	...	...		...
Oxford Road {arr.	...	...	...	...			7.38	...	...	7 0	...	...	...	S	...
{dep.	...	...	...	...	5 10			...	...	7 20	...	...	...		...
Islip ... ... ,,	...	4 52	...	...	5 17		Bills,	7 17	...	...	...	9 28	...	...	...
Oddington ... ,,	...	...	...	...	5 21		Padbury	...	...	...	...	...	...	...	...
Charlton ... ,,		...	...	...	5 26		7.27,	...	...	No. 1	...	...	...	...	...
Wendlebury ... ,,	Live Stock.	...	...	...	5 32		dep.	7 28	...	Bletchley	...	9 40		...	...
Bicester {arr.		5 3	...	...	5 37		Public	7 28	...	Arrives 8.50 p.m.	...		To Nuneaton.	...	
{dep.		5 4	...	...			+	7 30	...		...			...	...
Launton ... ,,	...	5 10	...	...	...			7 36	...		...			...	...
Marsh Gibbon & P. ,,	...	5 16	...	...	...			7 43	...		...			...	...
Charndon B'dge {arr.	...	...	...	...	...			...	...		...			...	...
Milk Stage {dep.	...	...	...	...	...			...	...		...			...	...
Claydon ... ,,	...	5 25	...	...	...			7 52	...		...			...	...
BANBURY ...dep.	3 20	...	4 40	4 55	...	...	6 40	...	6 55		7 15	...	...	...	...
Munition Sdg. ,,	...	...	...	...	...		...	...	...		...	...	...	...	...
Farthinghoe ... ,,	...	...	4 49	5 4	...		6 49	...	...		...	...	...	...	...
Cockley Brake J. ,,	3§32	...	4§53	5§ 8	...		6§53	...	7§10		7§32	...	...	...	...
Brackley {arr.	3 42	...	5 1	...	...		7 1	...	...		7 47	...	To Nuneaton.	...	
{dep.	4 20	...	5 5	...	...	6 32	7 5	...	...		8 0	...		...	...
Fulwell and W. ,,	...	...	5 13	...	...	6 40	7 12	...	...		...	...		...	...
Buckingham {arr.	4 35	...	5 23	...	...	6 50	7 22	...	...		8 20	...		...	...
{dep.	4 40	...	5 33	...	...	6 52	7+35	...	...		8 35	...		...	...
Padbury ... ,,	...	...	5 39	...	...	6 58	7+41	...	...		...	...		...	...
Verney Junc. {arr.	4 50	5 29	5 44	...	...	7 3	7 46	7 56	...		8 50	...		...	...
{dep.	4 55	5 32	5 46	...	...	7 5	7 48	7 59	...		9 0	...		...	...
Winslow... ... {arr.	5 0	5 37	5 51	...	...	7 10	7 53	8 4	...	8 20	9 10	...	12L 5	12L45	
{dep.	5 20	5 40	5 56	...	...	7 13	7 57	8 7	...	8 25	9 50	...	12 10	12 50	
Swanbourne ... ,,	...	5 45	6 1	...	...	7 18	8 2	8 15	...	...	...	...	...	...	
BLETCHLEY J. arr.	5 45	5 56	6 12	...	...	7 29	8 13	8 26	...	9 20	10 20	...	12 50	1 30	...

SUNDAYS.	1	2	3	4	5	6	7	8	9	10	11	12	13	14	15
			Milk.		Milk.	Pass.	Pass.		Express Goods.						
			a.m.		a.m.	p.m.	p.m.	p.m.							
OXFORD ... ...dep.	...	...	...	...			3 40			...	...	...	...	...	...
Port Meadow ... ,,	...	...	...	...			...			...	...	...	...	...	...
Wolvercote ... ,,	...	...	...	...	8.37, 8.58 a.m.		...			...	...	...	...	...	...
Oxford Road {arr.	...	...	...	...	Claydon		...			...	...	...	...	...	...
{dep.	...	...	...	...	8.22,		...			...	...	...	...	...	...
Islip ... ... ,,	...	...	...	...	Gibbon		3 53			...	...	...	...	...	...
Oddington ... ,,	...	...	...	...	Marsh		...		Cattle.	...	...	...	...	...	...
Charlton ... ,,	...	...	...	...	8.14,		...		Conveys	...	...	...	...	...	...
Wendlebury ... ,,	...	...	...	...	Launton		...			...	...	...	...	...	...
Bicester {arr.	...	...	...	...	Arr. Swanbourne		4 4			...	...	...	...	...	...
{dep.	...	...	...	...	8 10		4 6			...	...	...	...	...	...
Launton ... ,,	...	...	...	...	8 17		...			...	...	...	...	...	...
Marsh Gibbon & P. ,,	...	...	...	...	8 25		4 17			...	...	...	...	...	...
Charndon B'dge {arr.	...	...	...	...	8 30		...			...	...	...	...	...	...
Milk Stage {dep.	...	...	...	...	8 33		...			...	...	...	...	...	...
Claydon ... ,,	...	...	...	...	8 39		4 25			...	...	...	...	...	...
BANBURY ...dep.	...	...	...	...		3 20			8 0	...	...	...	...	...	...
Munition Sdg. ,,	...	...	...	...					...	...	...	...	...	...	...
Farthinghoe ... ,,	...	...	...	...	4.15.		3§33		8§13	...	...	...	...	...	...
Cockley Brake J. ,,	...	...	...	...	Gibbon		3§33		8§13	...	...	...	...	...	...
Brackley... {arr.	...	...	...	...	Marsh		...		8 25	...	...	...	...	...	...
{dep.	...	...	...	...	and		3 42		8 35	...	...	...	...	...	...
Fulwell & W. ,,	...	...	...	...	3.51		3 50		...	...	...	...	...	...	...
Buckingham {arr.	...	...	...	...	Islip		3 59		9 0	...	...	...	...	...	...
{dep.	...	...	7 20	...	Arrives		4 7		9 15	...	...	...	...	...	...
Padbury ... ,,	...	...	7 29	...			4 15		...	...	...	...	...	...	...
Verney Junc. {arr.	...	...	7 34	...			4 20		...	...	...	...	...	...	...
{dep.	...	...	...	...			4 35		9§30	...	...	...	...	...	...
Winslow ... {arr.	...	...	...	...	8 49		4 40		...	...	...	...	...	...	...
{dep.	...	...	...	...	8 54		4 45		...	...	...	...	...	...	...
Swanbourne ... ,,	...	...	...	...	9 0		4 53		...	...	...	...	...	...	...
BLETCHLEY J. arr.	...	...	...	...	9 5		5 5		10 5	...	...	...	...	...	...

Single Line, Banbury to Verney Junction—Electric Train Staff Stations—Banbury, Cockley Brake Junction, Brackley, Buckingham, and Verney Junction.

Banbury in 1930, showing the brisk goods traffic. A little of the large timber goods shed can be seen on the left. At this time it was handling a great deal of corn from Brackley and Farthinghoe to be delivered to the flour mill of Clarke's (Banbury) Ltd., Est. 1911. See Station Mills (Flour) on page 47 of 1922 survey.

L. & G.R.P.

only remaining evidence of the station's existence today, being used by British Road Services.

By 1938 the LMS were planning to take matters a stage further in their phasing out of Merton Street for passenger and parcels. The two companies decided to rebuild the Banbury stations as one complete unit situated with an access on the road bridge north of the present GWR station, with escalators to and from the platforms. The Buckinghamshire line would then be relaid around the gasworks forming a new junction just south of the existing GWR station; Merton Street as a passenger station would then of course be defunct. The outbreak of the second world war in 1939 ensured that the plan would not be implemented until the late 1950's when entirely different plans were drawn up for the rebuilding of the Great Western station only. Platform 4 of this station, a bay platform, was designed out of consideration for the Buckinghamshire line and there was some talk of running over the exchange siding into it but there is no evidence that this ever took place.

At the outbreak of World War Two Banbury was subjected to the restrictions familiar to all localities of strategic importance. The rail network was utilised to the maximum and all kinds of restrictions that did not endanger life and limb were temporarily suspended on the Buckinghamshire line, with long troop trains coming and going in every direction. The area was surrounded with airfields and army camps.

One sensitive area of the town was the Alcan Extrusions plant which began to produce the sheet metal for aircraft, and it could well have been as a result of this factory's occupation that the town was visited by a lone enemy raider in 1940. Without warning the Dornier circled the crowded town in broad daylight with the townspeople moving out of its path like quicksilver, running into shops and jumping under any convenient cover. A string of bombs fell diagonally across the gasworks and Great Western lines with the shrapnel and splinters scattering over a wide area. Several casualties, some fatal were inflicted upon the Great Western mess room where some workmen were carrying out repairs; the miracle was that the casualties were not in hundreds. The most spectacular effect of the raid was the direct hit upon a new gasholder which exploded with a great belch of yellow flame leaving other holders and installations covered in streams of gaseous fire each varying according to the size of the puncture. A piece of rail from the GWR smashed through the roof of a building quarter of a mile away. For the work of a single aircraft the mischief was extensive and psychologically alarming, no doubt some very strong questions were raised as to the early warning system's vulnerability. On one particular night in 1942 the station and gasworks were 'captured' by the British Army who celebrated the result of their success by setting up the ubiquitous tea urn upon the station forecourt. Another operation by the Royal Engineers

Driver and 2—4—2 tank pose in wartime Banbury watched by the crew of a 4F on the adjoining platform. Painting of the station roof appears to have ended rather abruptly, perhaps the painter was called to the forces. Facing the open door of the coach is an interesting little vehicle, a tricycle carrier.

L. & G.R.P.

The darkening hours – Banbury on a frosty morning in March 1941, vehicle restrictions have obviously been waived to bring in this train of troops and armoured vehicles. Some local units appear to be forming a kind of reception committee. The still damaged gas holder in the distance bears witness to the

It is interesting to relate that the three photographs shown here concerning the arrival of this light armoured unit in Banbury are in fact 'stills' from a film completed after the war and made by the LMS. The film, called 'Carrying the Load', narrated by Frank Phillips was a genuine documentary, therefore this is not a 'staged' setting.

North Eastern flat wagon, wooden planks have been placed along the entire train to drive the vehicles along. The peculiar brick structure behind the lamp is the goods shed, an ugly replacement for the L.N.W.R. timber building by the L.M.S. and as the only surviving example of the station, a rather unfair monument.

British Railways

L M . & S. TRAIN TIMETABLE

BANBURY TO BLETCHLEY.

UP.	WEEK DAYS.			TH & SAT.	SUNDAYS		
	am	pm	pm	pm	pm	am	pm
BANBURY dep.	7 20	2 25		3 40	7 0	7 56	3 2
Farthinghoe	7 27	2 32		3 48	7 7	—	—
Brackley	7 39	2 45	4 0	4 0	7 20	8 15	3 4
Fulwell and Westbury.........	7 50	2 53	4 6	4 6	7 28	8 25	3 4
Buckingham	8 1	3 4	4 21	4 21	7 42	8 37	4
Padbury	8 6	3 9	4 26	4 26	7 47	8 42	4
Verney Junction arr.	8 12	3 15	4 32	4 32	7 53	8 48	4 1
Verney Junction dep.	8 18	3 16	4 33	4 33	7 57	8 49	4 1
Winslow.........................	8 22	3 21	4 43	4 43	8 2	8 53	4 2
Swanbourne	8 27	3 25	4 48	4 48	8 8	8 57	4 2
BLETCHLEY arr..............	8 37	3 35	5 1	5 1	8 17	9 7	4 3

DOWN.	WEEK DAYS.		TH & SAT.	SUNDAYS	
	am	pm	pm	pm	pm
BLETCHLEY dep.	8 9	1 57	1 57	5 5	1
Swanbourne	8 19	2 5	2 5	5 15	1 1
Winslow..	8 26	2 10	2 10	5 21	1 2
Verney Junction arr.	8 31	2 15	2 15	5 26	1 2
Verney Junction dep.	8 34	2 16	2 16	5 27	1 2
Padbury	8 39	2 21	2 21	5 32	1 3
Buckingham	8 49	2 29	2 29	5 40	1 4
Fulwell and Westbury.........................	9 1	2 38	2 38	5 49	1 5
Brackley	9 8	2 44	2 44	5 55	1 5
Farthinghoe	9 25	—	2 57	6 7	—
BANBURY arr...............................	9 33		3 4	6 15	2 1

BANBURY, BLISWORTH AND NORTHAMPTON.

WEEK DAYS.			WEEK DAYS.	
	am	pm		am
BANBURY (Merton St. d.	1040	5 0	**NORTHAMPTON** (Castle) dep	9 0
Farthinghoe	1049	5 9	**Blisworth**	9 20
Helmdon	11 2	5 22	Towcester arr.	9 28
Wappenham	1112	5 31	Towcester dep.	9 30
Towcester arr.	1120	5 40	Wappenham	9 40
Towcester dep.	1121	5 41	Helmdon......................	9 49
Blisworth arr..............	**1130**	**5 51**	Farthinghoe	10 1
NORTHAMPTON (Castle)	1150	6 5	**BANBURY** arr.	10 9

No Sunday Trains.   No Sunday Trains.

The 1939-45 wartime time-table for Banbury became simplified in this page from a small booklet produced by the *Banbury Guardian*.

involved them with the erection of a pontoon style bridge completely covering the railway road bridge.

An example of train working during the war is contained within the railway timetable produced by the Banbury Guardian. The 8.9 would arrive in Banbury at 9.33, usually in the charge of a Stanier 2-6-4 tank, after running round the train and shunting it back into the train shed, the next job would be to give assistance to a twenty wagon train of ironstone from Wroxton to Wellingborough as far as Cockley Brake. On returning to the station, after taking water it would then carry out shunting tasks in the station area before returning to Bletchley with the 2.25 passenger.

After the cessation of hostilities Merton Street declined even further in passenger carrying receipts but thanks to Midland Marts strong agricultural developments the small station staff were kept busy with cattle and ore trains. One of the last signalmen to work in the Banbury box was a Mr T. Sharman who started there in 1947; his father had been porter and shunting guard at this station for forty years, often helping out at nearby Farthinghoe. Mr Sharman described to me a normal week when they handled about 200 cattle vans, sorted on arrival and despatched as and when required beginning with the sheep fair on Tuesday and the T.T. cattle on Wednesday. Thursday is the normal market day in Banbury with its familiar local bustle when two train loads of cattle left for Blisworth and Bletchley. Friday involved the movement of Irish cattle brought over the exchange sidings from the Western. He told me that on any one of these days they could be working from a normal shift up to one or two o'clock in the morning. This pace was maintained in varying degrees until the early sixties when British Railways began to phase out this kind of traffic altogether and left Merton Street without a cause, in weedy dereliction. But much was still to happen in the final fifteen years, which I have reserved for a later chapter.

Light engine to leave Bletchley at 6.0 p.m. (Sundays), for Banbury :—						
			dep. p.m.		arr. p.m.	dep. p.m.
Bletchley	...	...	... 6 0	Brackley	—	6§47
Verney Junction	...	...	... 6§20	Cockley Brake Junction	—	6§57
Buckingham	...	...	... 6§31	Banbury	7 10	—
				(1978—Commenced August 28)		

Excerpt from L.N.W.R. working time-table of 1922. Heavy cattle shipments seemed to require this extra working.

J. Lowe

After bringing the 5.28 from Bletchley into the opposite platform, No. 80083 propels the stock out to the loop in order that she may run round. The empty stock is then pushed into what was often considered the S.M.J. platform, this will now form the 7.0 p.m. to Bletchley. The engine uncouples to go and turn on the old L.N.W.R. turntable, most engine crews would rather run a tank engine in conventional position than bunker first. Instructions by British Railways issued at that time that all turning should be done on the Western Region turntable were largely ignored, not for any partisan reasons, simply that many Bletchley men did not know the 'road' and this would require a Western engine as pilot, not to mention the 'hanging about'. How irresistible it always seemed to young and old alike to watch as the train was re-coupled, even though one would see the same operation carried out many times, like the boy in the photograph watching the fireman.

W.A. Camwell

Banbury (Merton Street) in March 1952. 2-6-4T No. 42669 prepares to depart with a Bletchley train. The condition of the station reflects the slender passenger services that were still in use. It was almost the end, the Blisworth trains having ceased the year before. Staple goods traffic is evident with ore and cattle vehicles.

H.C. Casserley

A scene on 19th May 1951. Stanier tank No. 42669 prepares to leave with the 3.45 to Bletchley. In the customary ex-S.M.J. platform No. 43520 ex-Midland 3F has a lengthy wait with the 4.45 Towcester and Blisworth. The station does appear rather down-at-heel on this photograph and two years later the roof was removed for safety reasons.

W.A. Camwell

Last train to Blisworth with a lively 4F in charge, a single coach not overburdened with ceremony. Note replacement of gas lamps after nationalisation but the old L.N.W.R. yard lamp on the right has endured.

L. & G.R.P.

Farthinghoe station circa 1905. Mr Tustain, the Stationmaster, looks along the platform toward Banbury.

The interesting gothic lettering used for this chapter heading is taken from the cover of the Passenger Record Book at Farthinghoe and reduced to fit this page. It is believed to have been the work of Jim Brown as the book is the one in use from 1946 until the station's closure.

L. & G.R.P

Farthinghoe

Chapter Four

Farthinghoe

This was the next station to Banbury being only 3½ miles from the terminus on a 1 in 120 gradient rising towards Cockley Brake. The exact day it was opened is not known but it was almost certainly within the opening year of the line. A letter from Henry Tancred, M.P. to a certain William Munton, dated 19th July, 1850 mentioned the suggested appointment of one William Tustain as Messenger for the Post Office in Banbury, from the Buckinghamshire Railway to Middleton Cheney, a village nearby. On that evidence it would appear that the station was not yet in service.

Before the miniature electric train staff was brought into use on the branch on 14th September, 1890 Farthinghoe was a separate block post working up and down signals operated from a ground frame. There has never been more than the one siding, trailing from the up side. It is an isolated spot being over a mile to the north-west of the village of its name, but roughly central for serving the two other nearby villages of Greatworth and Middleton Cheney. This station, like Banbury was of all timber construction with the exception of the brick-built Stationmaster's house which was behind the station buildings and was quite an imposing structure. The station lost its own Stationmaster in 1930 when it came directly under the control of Banbury. The last man to fill this post was coincidentally also called Tustain; he kept twenty bee hives in the station garden. Originally he had been assisted by a young porter called Harold Chester who left for the first world war. His place was taken by a Mr Pease who remained in solitary employment on the station when Mr Tustain left. Stationmaster Tustain had a reputation for indulging in harmless practical jokes should any opportunity arise. One such opportunity came when once he was walking along a train in Farthinghoe that was waiting to leave for Brackley, passengers for Farthinghoe having already left the station. Looking inside one of the empty compartments he saw a plain brown paper parcel left on the luggage rack, naturally he removed the parcel from the train to be placed in the safety of the station, thence to seek its owner. He noticed that the parcel carried a local address and so he decided to enquire at this address when going off duty. He did not have to wait very long before a breathless gentle-

Farthinghoe in 1930; but for L.M.S. on the porter's trolley little has changed from the former company. The siding appears to be enjoying some brisk employment, delivery of coal for Palmers perhaps, or a supply of pink roadstone ballast.

L. & G.R.P.

man came running back onto the platform, and became upset on seeing that the train had departed. He explained the loss to Mr Tustain who listened thoughtfully and then replied, "I'll get on to Brackley and see if they can wire it back to us". The man eyed Tustain curiously, but was prepared to settle for anything that would return his travelling parcel. Mr Tustain then took a few moments for a quick aside to Harold Chester. He then asked the gentleman to follow him to the telegraph and witness the miraculous process take place. After a few moments on the line he turned and beamed at the quizzical passenger explaining that, "They caught it at Brackley and they're sending it straight down the wire." By now the man must have been forming some kind of belief that the LNWR promoted lunatics in charge of their stations until Mr Tustain took him down the platform and pointed to the telegraph pole where his precious parcel was now hanging by its string, looking for all the world as if it had been swept along the wire. Mr Tustain asked Chester to retrieve the parcel. Both men carried out the whole operation courteously, as if it was

Harold Chester, L.N.W.R. Farthinghoe.

Harry Somerton

quite a normal procedure. The poor chap left the station clutching his parcel and staring at the telegraph wires and continually shaking his head in disbelief. By the time he was out of sight and sound it is probable that the two rogues had to hold each other up, celebrating with convulsive laughter the success of their prank.

The station of Farthinghoe must have known a great deal of laughter, especially that of children for often the children of Mr Haslop rode up on the railway to the station and played with Mr Tustain's children in the large garden, between watching each train come and go. They would end their day with an enjoyable country tea around a large table in the station house, before returning to Banbury. Up to the mid-1930's goods trains would shunt the siding daily and there were regular loads of a pink roadstone granite unloaded there besides the coal of Palmers Colliery merchants. The stone began to cease during that decade and

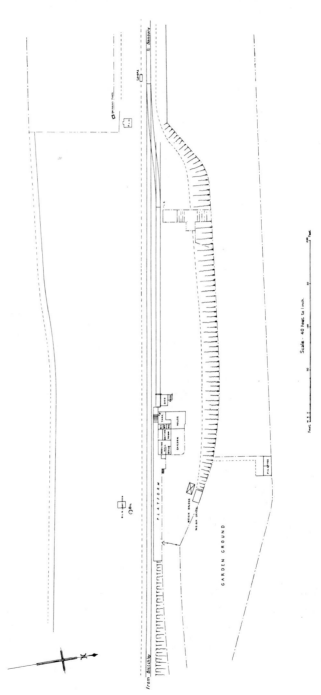

L. M. & S. R. FARTHINGHOE

RATING PLAN

Scale - 40 Feet to 1 inch.

Track plan at Farthinghoe with details of buildings.

Farthinghoe at time of closure, looking toward Banbury. The peculiar indentation in the timber platform and fence was due to unloading and loading of heavy milk churns from the same spot.

Farthinghoe looking toward Bletchley at time of closure.

Len's of Sutton

goods traffic dwindled until some wartime requirements of the R.A.F. involved unloading ammunition at Farthinghoe destined for Hinton-in-the-Hedges; the coal continued up to the station's closure for goods.

One of the most interesting characters to occupy the one-man station in later years was Jim Brown, who seemed to enjoy his lonely life in the country station and was a prolific gardener. His horticultural skill was a great surprise and joy to the passing traveller on a warm and hazy June day. He grew all his own fresh fruit and vegetables in the commodious station garden; appreciative enginemen would often receive the opportunity to sample thereof. As he seldom went into any of the villages or left the station at all, he was to most people regarded as something of a recluse. Those that saw him most would be the platelayers and line gangs who hinted that the shiny buttons and battered railway uniform concealed a character of inordinate wealth. Probably an exaggerated view for a man who had found satisfaction in an idyllic life. When the line to Towcester was closed Jim Brown would surprise and amuse the passengers of any train that came to rest at his station by calling out the names of these non-existent stations along that branch as if they were still in use. When the station did close to passengers in November 1952, Jim Brown endured, working the station as if it was still in service, which for the goods trains it still was, until the line's final closure in 1963. His final whereabouts became difficult to ascertain as his presence seemed to fade from the station as it became more derelict and the gardens overgrown, until the structures were removed altogether and ignominiously replaced by a council dump and pulveriser plant. I cannot imagine a cruder comparison for what had once been a railway pastoral scene.

L.N.W.R. vintage between Banbury and Farthinghoe, original company stile crossing, evidence of which exists only on the Banbury extension.
Brian Garland

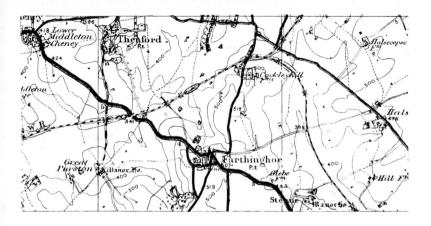

Chapter Five

Cockley Brake

The only other junction on the branch beside Verney, in the original survey for building the line the plans had included a tunnel through the hill at Cockley Brake (510 yds). As the company became more cost conscious the plan was dropped in favour of the cheaper alternative of a higher level cutting, making it the highest point of the branch, levelling off from a one in one hundred and twenty climb from Banbury. At Cockley Brake the assisting locomotive of any particular heavy goods train from Banbury would have completed its task and would be released to return to the terminus five and a quarter miles away. The layout of the junction included a short loop to hold passing trains and exchange of staff token. Cockley Brake did not become a junction until the opening of the Northampton and Banbury line on the 1st June, 1872 the details of which are included in the Banbury chapter.

Memories of Cockley Brake seem to be more easily recollected by railwaymen in the inclement conditions of winter, as this bleak location was often affected in much the same way as parts of that famous line between Settle and Carlisle, when even moderate falls of snow would produce enormous drifting. It is recorded that in 1881 Cockley Brake was under snow and the line was closed, and in the deluge of 1947 a passenger train became stuck fast in the cutting whilst the p.w. men shovelled for two days to remove it. Assisting them were two 0-8-0 G2's despatched from Bletchley, they in turn were nearly to suffer the same fate until they wrenched the forlorn train from its icy grip and the 'Brake' closed behind them under the steadily falling snow, abandoned until the thaw.

Probably the longest serving signal man at the 'Brake' was William Henry Somerton who was born in 1874. His early railway service began by working on the construction of the Great Central Railway before becoming a porter at Brackley, LNWR. He took up his position in the

William Henry Somerton takes up his position as Signalman at the old Cockley
Brake box; he stands at the top of the steps whilst the signalman of some years,
Mr Bird, is standing in the doorway. They were to work the two shifts at the box.
The peculiar bird cage structure on the wall of the box between them is just that
Mr. Somerton and Mr Bird were 'linnet fanciers'. The three gentlemen with the
gangers 'lorry' are Mr. Williams, Mr. Trinder — the man with the flag is not known.
The box is a very early example of an L.N.W.R. box and would have been installed
with the building of the junction with the Northampton & Banbury. On this
evidence it is not unreasonable to suppose that the first box at Banbury was not
dissimilar.

Harry Somerton

Mr. Bird operating the old box at Cockley Brake, where he took up his duties in
1901 after working at Winslow station. Very much a countryman Mr. Bird was a
keen horticulturist, unable to resist brightening up the interior of the box with
plants around the window sill. He also became enthusiastic about Bee keeping
after much influence from Mr. Tustain. He retired from the railway company at
Cockley Brake in 1922. He died on the 30th May 1939 aged 82 years.

William Henry Somerton stands outside his new box, opened in 1922. This is the
L.N.W.R. type 5 signal box introduced after 1904.

Harry Somerton

Cockley Brake Junction with line to Blisworth turning left and Bletchley to the
right, early 1930's.

L. & G.R.P.

box at Cockley Brake in 1903 retiring in 1939 only to be asked to
return in 1940 for the wartime emergency, when he did finally retire he
had completed forty years on the branch spanning the days of the
Northampton and Banbury and Stratford and Midland Junction and of
course the LNWR and LMS. His son told me that he was a keen
railwayman and even after his retirement he would visit the box and
help to defrost the points, in summer he would continue to tend the
'Box garden' with its much favoured gooseberry bushes in the place
where he had worked nearly all his life. He died in September, 1955 at
the ripe age of 81. The shifts at the box in 1911 would be for twelve

Mr Somerton and Mr Bird in 1912, without the linnets this time. Addition of a
lucky horseshoe has been nailed — unluckily, upside down. An interesting comparison with the earlier photograph shows a number of trees in the background of
Cockley wood have now been moved. By the time that the last signalbox was
dismantled descendants had recovered their former profusion, as indeed they
remain today.

Harry Somerton

No. 16A of the Stratford-upon-Avon & Midland Junction Railway poses with its train of three L.N.W.R. six-wheelers outside the new box at Cockley Brake. This clear view of the depth beneath the carriage doors of these vehicles leads one to imagine that alighting and boarding the train at Banbury and Farthinghoe platforms which were no more than two feet high, even with the aid of the platform steps, must have been a precarious business.

Harry Somerton

hours overlapping. The first man started at 4.00 am and would be relieved by the second man at 10.00 am. The first man would then go to work on sundry duties at Farthinghoe leaving the second man in charge of the box until 10.00 pm, the first having returned to sign off from the box at 4.00 pm. This operated on a weekly alternate basis.

During the period of the ammunition trains Mr Bird, the signalman on the opposite shift to Mr Somerton, witnessed the alarming sight of a long train of explosives passing by with a tarpaulin wagon cover ablaze, possibly caused by a spark from the locomotive. Prompt action at Brackley prevented a conflagration too horrendous to contemplate.

The line to Blisworth or the 'old crab and winkle' as Bletchley men called it was closed in 1951 and the rails were taken up in 1953. The signal box was closed and the block section extended to between Banbury and Brackley.

Today the spot is a haven of bird song between the slow grazing fields with a few traces of mossy rubble to suggest that there was ever such a thing as a signalbox. The diverging lines of a once double-junction are now two narrow woodland paths; it does not seem possible to believe, were it not a fact, that the 18″ goods once panted up the hill, or the hurrying 2-4-2 tank caused these trees to vibrate as it faded away with its rake of maroon and white coaches. Such is the way of nature, to quietly conceal so many active years.

Skew Bridge at the turn of the century. Additional buttressing has been built on the side that would originally have held up the line, had one been built.

A.N. Emmerson Collection

A Webb 2-4-2T hurries under Skew Bridge and on its way to Banbury. The vehicle next to the engine is a horsebox, this scene being at the turn of the century.

A.N. Emmerson Collection

Chapter Six

Brackley

The old town of Brackley is some fourteen miles along the branch from Verney, the station was opened for service on the same day as the line itself. The name is derived from a description of nearby fields that formerly abounded in fern and bracken. It is seated on rising ground near the river Ouse and consists principally of one wide street nearly a mile in length. The town is only just within the south-western extremity of the county of Northamptonshire, and had, in 1850, a population of some 2,277 people employed in traditional country industries, supported by the surrounding farms.

The LNWR station was located at the southern end of the main street and was attractively constructed, not in the more familiar iron-stone but in a yellow-grey coloured stone that is probably even more localised. Some quarries at Croughton are not as old as the line but the likeness of the material there makes it reasonable to suppose that it came from the same area. Eight miles divide Buckingham from Brackley, where the branch passes through four miles and one furlong of the parish. There can be little doubt that, as one would expect, the railway brought an increased prosperity to the small scale commerce of the town. By 1874, when George Wallis was station master, there were two separate banking houses established in the community and two success-ful breweries therein, with a good broad basis of shopkeepers to supply the local needs. Notwithstanding this, the small town of Brackley never outgrew its rural charm, even though the stations of two great railways have come and gone; for in 1898 the Great Central opened their main

William Henry Somerton (in straw hat) says his farewell to Brackley staff; the Stationmaster is on the extreme right. Striking view of two very unusual gas lamps with clear glass-filled lantern head, this is the only example like this seen on the branch. Note the cast lettering 'BRACKLEY' has been removed above opening in entrance way.

Brackley c. 1902, there is a Sunday look about this scene, with men working on the line and the two smart gentlemen on the right. Note the cast iron lettering 'BRACKLEY' above the station portico, this had not long been removed on the previous photograph.

A.N. Emmerson Collection

Late 1920's at Brackley, still very L.N.W.R. The signal box at Brackley is like the original box at Buckingham, a type four L.N.W.R. dating from 1870 up to 1904. The massive cattle-crossing bridge in the distance was demolished sometime around 1930.

line station at the north end of the town and must have drawn a great deal of trade away from the LNWR company's monopoly as the Great Central had a faster and more direct route to London.

Brackley LNWR was built to a familiar pattern for a medium size branch line station, a single loop enclosed between two facing platforms, but it was not without its own curiosities. The platform was of the antique height of thirty-two inches, a characteristic of the Banbury branch. One interesting feature was the water tank which supplied the engines from a single column, as well as some of the station requirements. This was situated in the roof of the stone shelter on the up side of the line (see photograph), a neat piece of integration. It was refilled from a nearby spring, the only problem being that once an engine has been re-plenished from this limited reservoir it would be some time before the slowly refilling tank would be adequate to supply another. Another and possibly frustrating feature of the station was the example of the LNWR's penchant for wagon turntables, the goods shed was thus built at right angles to the line. A slight gradient enabled the vehicles to roll easily from the table into the shed, but manhandling them back onto the turn-table was quite another matter. Probably the most striking feature of the station was the delivery line to the brewery of Hopkins and Norris whose premises were situated on the higher part of the town. The line left the

Brackley 1950.

station sharply to the right as one approached from Buckingham and climbed a severe gradient of one in twenty. People who have some memory of this spur, and refer to it as the 'barrel line' tell me that they never saw any other form of traction used other than that of horses drawing the wagons up this steep gradient to be gravity shunted on their return to the station yard, it is little wonder that a trap was installed at the bottom of this slope! Sid Sellers, signalman at Brackley in 1928 remembers that the line was deep in weeds at that time and although Hopkins and Norris were still flourishing and still using the station with dray and horse, they ceased to use the spur early in that decade. It appears that the actual lifting of the rails took place in the first few years of the 1930's. A signalman who operated the box in 1890 spoke of the intense activity at Brackley with the arrival of the Great Central Railway. A new siding was installed near the ten-mile post and heavy trainloads of bricks were brought up from Buckingham to be offloaded there. The ground frame for the sidings was locked by Annett's key which was released from the signal box. The 'barrel line' still appears to be in use on the ordnance maps of 1922, but I am told it was completely lifted by 1935; the brewery remained in business for many years afterwards. The building is now used by Bromley's soap works.

On the Buckinghamshire Railway documents of 1846 showing the proposed route of the line and deviation, there is the following statement: 'Passing the cemetery at Brackley the top of the rails are three hundred and thirty feet thirty-four inches below the upper surfaces of the stone sill of the doorway of the chapel in the burial ground called the lower end burial ground.' This was the datum for the line, a level intended to be parallel with the intended junction at Banbury. The chapel was in the lower burial ground of the church of St. James and was immediately alongside the line opposite the main station buildings. This chapel fell derelict and was finally demolished. When I visited the area it seemed to me rather touching to see the tilted and abandoned gravestones practically concealed by the long grass, with two large warehouses standing on the spot where the church used to be, albeit they have a tasteful stone finish.

To find Brackley's finest hour, or day we must return to a date in 1950, the thirteenth of May, when the town was in a state of great excitement for the arrival at Brackley ex-LNWR station of His Majesty King George VI who was to pass through the station on his way to Silverstone and the first Grand Prix d'Europe. This was indeed a great day for the Station Master, Mr Whitney, who would traditionally receive the first reigning monarch to travel the line in its history. The Royal train was in the charge of two resplendent 'Black Fives' and their Bletchley engine crews. It was a day well suited to the occasion for the sightseers that crowded the edge of the line in the warm May sunshine. A curious silence reigned, electric with apprehension, as the onlookers viewed the silent thread of rail that had been cleared of every conceiv-

His Majesty King George VI steps from the Royal train at Brackley to be received by Mr. Whitney. Note the old ammunition box that became a royal step.

Mrs. Whitney

Mr. Whitney stands before the two resplendent 'Black Fives' that brought the Royal Train in 1950. He was Station Master at Brackley from 1949 to 1956, in that year he took the same post at Buckingham from where he retired in 1959.

Mrs Whitney

able obstacle and prepared for the time when many would have their first glimpse of the monarch. Signals were pulled off and when the first sound of the train became apparent murmurs of excitement rippled through the crowds. Into this arena strode the two shining 'Black Fives'; in the prime of condition they drew alongside the station with the merest whisper of exhausting steam. The reception committee including noble personages and civic dignitaries were lined up along the modest platform led by Mr Whitney; around them the pink and white apple blossom accorded the Royal visitors with a characteristic country welcome. There was one moment of concern however, when it was discovered that the platform at Brackley was lower than usual beneath the steps of the saloon from which their Majesties were to alight; a wooden case was hurriedly produced and placed before the step, unfortunately as the photograph shows there was not sufficient time to acquire the customary material that would regally conceal the use of the box. Nevertheless this did not in any way mar the wonderful occasion for this small Northamptonshire town. Wives of the local railwaymen of Brackley and Buckingham were given special permission to be on the platform where they could watch the arrival of the Royal train, otherwise the area of the station was closely cordoned off from the public by railway and county police. The Queen was wearing a two piece suit of rich powder blue with a feather trimmed hat, whilst Princess Margaret was wearing 'dusty' pink with a closely fitting feathered hat to match.

The whole town was bedecked as never before with the separate school uniforms of Magdalen College School and the High School smartly in evidence; one striking spectacle seen from a distance were the yellow caps worn by the boys of Beechborough School, Westbury. The unstinting loyalty of the town could never have been more marked than this great display of red, white and blue streamers, bunting and shimmering lines of roadside flags, as the glossy limousine glided away from the station and passed each section of the crowd.

Arthur Marriot and Sid Green, the two Brackley signalmen were both on duty that day and felt a justifiable pride that the unusually large train and its exceptional branch line motive power was handled with such consummate ease. Arthur came to the Brackley box in 1940 from the Oxford Road box of the Verney Junction — Oxford section. He has a long tradition on the Buckinghamshire railways as his father was a p.w. man of many years service. He remembered some of the darker days at Brackley when during the war Churchill tanks had been unloaded there. In the blackout, their drivers were unaware of their location as the operation was part of an exercise for forming up the vehicles under the cover of darkness in a hostile terrain. Sometimes the goods trains were run through to Banbury with 0-8-0 Midland 7F's and 2-8-0 'Austerity' class locos in charge, this must have been straining the regulations on locomotive working somewhat and could not have been too often as the track was not considered suitable for engines of this size. One amusing and recurring problem in some of the locomotive types that worked down the branch, which could not have been so humorous to the engine crews, was the obstinate behaviour of some of the Lancashire and Yorkshire 0-6-0 tender engines. Displaced from duties in the north, these engines would drift south into the Bletchley stud; though they became nicknamed 'Gracie Fields' they provided anything but a harmonious relationship with the enginemen. Arthur recalls that on a number of occasions when awaiting a train being hauled by one of these engines he would look from the box to see an inexplicable pall of black smoke that remained completely motionless some way down the line. Further inquiry would reveal that the fireman was laboriously removing the fire from the firebox and "chucking" it onto the lineside; the water injectors had refused to respond and so with regard to regulations he was taking the necessary precaution and emptying the fire. It was then necessary for another locomotive to either push or pull the recalcitrant 'Lanky' into the sidings. Peculiarly, when the engine had cooled the injectors began to work again, this did not endear them to the Bletchley enginemen. An exception was loco No. 12086 which was fitted with Gresham & Craven injectors and had a Belpaire firebox, this loco could be relied upon not to cause problems.

Brackley goods yard was not a large size but made the best of its shortcomings when traffic was busy, which could be a regular occurrence with a daily delivery to the gas works of anything from three to twelve wagons, whilst the brewery would require a regular four to five wagons of malt and sugar. The cattle dock was only capable of taking four vans at one unloading, and this on a line where a forty van cattle train was not considered exceptional. Northants farmers received substantial supplies of their cattle feed through the yard and Wiggins coal merchants were supplied daily; in all from the point of view of merchandise and livestock it was a fairly active life for a single line branch.

By 1956 the Brackley passenger service, like Banbury and Farthinghoe was hanging on a single thread and could well have snapped in that year had not the line been chosen for the British Railways railcar experiment which I have decided to deal with in a separate chapter, and was thus able to "soldier on" for four more years.

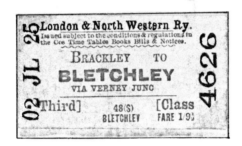

Pick-up goods leaving Banbury (Merton Street) in 1955. No. 80043 assists an ex-Midland 4F that is making the return working to Swanbourne sidings near Bletchley. A description of the tank engine's role is included on p. 69, the difference in this working being that the engine would now be required to go to Brackley to work a complete section as by this time the signal box at Cockley Brake had been closed. The buildings to the left of the train are the ex-GWR engine sheds.

Barrie Trinder

Bradshaw's time-table for 1922.

M. Morris Collection

Interesting photograph taken at Brackley between 1895 and 1901 of a Webb 2-2-2-2 Compound tank with 4' 6" driving wheels, No. 1967 original No. 687. Cylinders were 14" x 18" high and 26" x 24" low pressure; heating surface of 994 sq. ft., boiler pressure of 160 lb. sq. inch and weighed 50 tons 17 cwt. It was based on the 4' 6" 2-4-2 tank and worked for a time on the 'Outer Circle', Broad Street to Mansion House. For this it was fitted with condensing apparatus which some time after 1895 was removed and the side tanks cut short (as in the photograph).

In its early days it was nicknamed 'fore and aft' by that distinguished railway chronicler A.E. Ahrons, who regarded its peculiar and irritating reciprocations when moving from the station as rocking its train of passengers in the manner of a rowing eight. They were never popular and were regarded as Webb 'unmentionables'.

The Late W. Clark

Brackley L.M.S. looking toward Buckingham. Note the signs of L.M.S. ownership: name-board above signal box door, the chimney pots have been shortened and a plethora of small flower beds have sprung up along the platform.

Len's of Sutton

No. of Road Van.	Labelled TO	Trains worked by			Stations served.	Remarks.
		Time of Departure	From	To		

The days on which the Vans leave the Starting Point are shown in the Remarks column.

From Bedford

31	Bletchley	11 20 a.m.	Bedford	Bletchley	Millbrook, Ridgmont, Woburn Sands, Bletchley	Daily.
32	Cambridge ...	7 0 a.m.	Bedford	Cambridge	Blunham, Sandy, Potton, Gamlingay, Old North Road, Lord's Bridge, Cambridge	Daily.
		4 35 p.m.	Bedford	Cambridge		

From Birmingham (Curzon Street)

37	Brackley	10.30 p.m.	Curzon St.	Stechford	Swanbourne, Winslow, Verney Jct. and Met. Rly., Padbury, Buckingham, Fulwell & Westbury, Brackley	Daily.
		1 40 a.m.	Stechford	Bletchley		
		10 15 a.m.	Bletchley	Brackley		

From Bletchley

53	Brackley	10 15 a.m.	Bletchley	Brackley	Verney Jct., Padbury, Buckingham, Fulwell & Westbury, Brackley	Daily.
54	Bedford	7 30 a.m.	Bletchley	Bedford	Woburn Sands, Ridgmont, Millbrook, Bedford	Daily.
55	Cambridge ...	3 45 a.m.	Bletchley	Cambridge	Blunham, Sandy, Potton, Gamlingay, Old North Road, Lord's Bridge, Cambridge	Daily.
		1 35 p.m.	Bletchley	Bedford		
		4 35 p.m.	Bedford	Cambridge		
56	Luton	8 15 a.m.	Bletchley	Leighton	Leighton, Stanbridgeford, Dunstable, Luton	Daily.
		6 10 p.m.	Leighton	Dunstable		
		9 40 a.m.	Dunstable	Luton		

Working Appendix — Working of Road Vans.

L.M.S. — Cyril Gibbins

RESTRICTED NUMBER OF VEHICLES TO BE CONVEYED BY PASSENGER TRAINS OVER CERTAIN SECTIONS OF LINE.

Section.		Up or Down.	Restricted maximum number of bogie vehicles or their equivalent. *	Remarks.
From	To			
Coalport	Dawley & Stirchley	Either	5	Trains exceeding 5 actual vehicles must have a brake vehicle at each end. In the case of a motor train the engine may be in rear.
Dawley & Stirchley ...	Hadley Junction	,,	12	
Marton Junction ...	Weedon	,,	8 for ordinary trains / 13 for mixed trains	Between Leamington Spa and Daventry.
Nottingham ...	Market Harboro' ...	,,	13	—
Shackerstone Jn. ...	Loughboro'	,,	‡13	‡—Only 10 bogie vehicles or their equivalent between Shepshed and Coalville.
Banbury	Brackley	,,	7	—

Working Appendix, passenger loading restrictions.

Mr. C. Gibbins

Fairburn tank No. 42062 gets away briskly from Brackley with a Bletchley—Banbury train in the early 1950's.

W.A. Camwell

The 7.0 p.m. to Bletchley with No. 80083 at its head has now reached Brackley with steam to spare. Although the poster close to the porter has the British Railways 'sausage' motif the block lettering on the board still proclaims the L.M.S. whilst beyond the bridge the old L.N.W.R. 'home' signal nods approval, as it has done for nearly a century.

W.A. Camwell

Nearly complete bridge over the L.N.W.R. branch by the Great Central near Brackley in 1891. The rails in the foreground are the temporary siding laid in for the use of the new company, many brick trains were parked there.

A.N. Emmerson Collection

Where lines crossed. The ex-Great Central line above the ex-L.N.W.R. near Brackley, both removed by the time of this photograph in 1975. The old print above was taken from near the same spot.

Brian Garland

Chapter Seven

Fulwell and Westbury

Between Brackley and Buckingham are the only two gated level crossings
on the line; they are just over a mile apart, the closest to Brackley is at
Fulwell. The intersection is of a minor road from Fringford through to
Westbury which is a mile north of the site of the station, meeting at a
junction with the Brackley—Buckingham road. Fulwell and Westbury
was a modest station, consisting of a single low platform, a small ticket
office, W.C.'s, ladies waiting room and general waiting room, with
clock. The modesty of its dimensions gave it an added charm. It was a
neat timber structure facing the clean brushed gravel of a single platform that was smoothly edged with a row of curved bricks. On the
other side of the road was the Station Master's house, a position that
ceased to exist in 1930 with Mr Kirk, thenceforth coming under the
authority of Brackley. Behind the house was a short looped siding
controlled by a ground frame and electric token. All of the station area
was protected by signals with which the gates were interlocked, there
was also a cattle pen and loading gauge.

The LNWR did not see the necessity of a station here until 1879
when it was opened on the first of August in that year. As the Tingewick
Brass Band played 'Let the Hills Resound' the first train drew up; the
band followed this with 'My Grandfather's Clock' for the train from
Brackley. The opening of the station did not alter in the block working;
it was an intermediate station in the Buckingham and Brackley staff
section.

The 5.28 from Bletchley to Banbury arrives at Fulwell & Westbury on 7th August 1956, with No. 80083 in charge.

Fulwell & Westbury in 1960.

Len's of Sutton

The two gated crossings, the other being near Bacon's House, also feature in a signalling curiosity on the Banbury branch. In both the Buckingham and Brackley boxes an instrument was installed for working block indicating. This consisted of a 'train on line' needle which could pass on the information to receiving instruments at both of these crossings, within the 'block' both visually and audibly by a bell. This would of course warn the crossing-keeper of a train's departure from either direction.

During the 1930's the station was manned by two porters, Bill Bodsworth and Len Ewins. Primarily their jobs amounted to operating the gates, issuing tickets, controlling any shunting that was required in the siding, taking the wagon numbers and phoning them through to Bletchley. After supervising cattle through the small pen they would be required to trim hedges and all flora and fauna, sweep the station and keep it in good order. In addition they were responsible for balancing the books at the end of the day. By the late 1930's there were two porters running the station. Fred Kimble who lived in the commodious station house and Sid Green who lived at Syresham, cycling back and forth to work. In 1941 Sid Green was transferred to work at Brackley and his place at the station was taken by a local woman who lived in some cottages at Fulwell, overlooking the station. 'Dolly' Chapman became a great favourite with the engine crews and passengers; often proving that her dry humour could be more than a match for larky railwaymen; she recalled how Bill Bodsworth and Len Ewins had once hung her hat atop the signal when she was a girl. 'Dolly' soon proved that she was able to fill Sid Green's place by carrying out all the above-mentioned tasks to great satisfaction, besides chasing runaway goats up the platform and being locked in one of the vans by one of the guards and taken up to the cattle pen, to return on foot; the goats were secured in the waiting room. Before she began work on the station she recalled some of the good summers before the war when all of her relations, considerable in number, would come down to Fulwell for a day in the country on a 'Five Shilling Special'. Once in this beautiful Oxfordshire setting they would pick large quantities of blackberries and mushrooms, then spend the last leisurely hours of a beautiful day sitting in a large group in the garden, before the arrival of their return train down the line from Banbury.

There was of course an opposite side to life in this idyllic setting, when wartime realities reached even this country by-way. On one night 'Dolly' had to remain on duty all night to open the gates every two hours to allow heavily loaded trains of military equipment through the station, and going on duty at half past five on cold winter mornings to open the gates at six for the first train must have been a testing experience.

Fulwell and Westbury are friendly, easy going villages and 'Dolly' and all other villagers were much aggrieved to lose their highly personal contact with the railway, no more the waves from the engine crews to the cottages on the hill with cheeky schoolchildren doing their homework in the waiting room.

When the station closed to passengers on the second of January, 1961 the station buildings and station master's house fell derelict, although the final closure did not come until the second of December, 1963. The house was purchased and restored for occupation in 1968 by Mr and Mrs Boore who occupied the sidings yard and established their business of restoring vintage cars there. A new section has been carefully added to the house which has not in any way spoiled its LNWR profile, and is in excellent condition both outside and within where one is afforded an excellent view from the large windows both up and down the line. On examining the structure one soon becomes aware that it was built to easily withstand the close proximity of the trains and its present condition is a monument to its builder's ability.

Bacon's House crossing has no station, a single siding on the 'down' side and cattle landing was considered all that was necessary. It is in a very isolated spot on the road from Finmere to Water Stratford in deep lush countryside where the silence is only broken by the occasional passing tractor. The last occupants of the little crossing keeper's house were Mr and Mrs Faulkner, Mr Faulkner being a coal merchant and keeping his stocks in the yard whilst Mrs Faulkner was employed by the railway as crossing keeper. Today the house appears unoccupied with only a faint suggestion beneath the tall grass and small trees that anything of a siding was ever there at all, whilst the countryside has returned

Fulwell & Westbury looking toward Buckingham, a view photographed in June, 1957. The station is looking quite trim, probably in preparation for the railcar experiment. Note the 'Dow-Mac' concrete sleepers, a few were installed on the branch in 1946.

Mr. D. Thompson

to the bird-sung peace of a hundred and twenty-six years ago when a large army of railway workers felled the nearby woods, to hew and cut the timber that would be used in the building of the Buckinghamshire Railway.

Special instructions for manning of level crossing gates, Working Appendix 1922.

J. Lowe

Sunday Duty of Gatemen, Branch Lines.—In order that the Gatemen at the Level Crossings on the undermentioned branches may be relieved of Sunday duty as far as possible, it has been arranged for the gates to be placed across the line and kept open for the road traffic a Week-ends between the hours named in the following table, the signals during that time being kept at "Danger."

NAME OF BRANCH.	Gates to be first placed across the Line after the passing of Train named below.	Gates to be placed across the Road	After passing of Trains named in preceding column gates to be placed across the Line till hour named below, when ordinary mode of working the gates must be resumed.
Oxford.	2.0 a.m. Goods from Bletchley, and 3.40 p.m. passenger from Oxford.	20 minutes before Booked Passenger Trains.	4.0 a.m. Monday.
Banbury.	7.0 p.m. Passenger from Bletchley and 7.15 p.m. Goods from Banbury, Saturday.	20 minutes before Booked Trains.	5.0 a.m., Monday (except Fulwell and Westbury, where gates are across the line until 6.0 a.m.).
Cambridge.	10.45 p.m. Goods from Cambridge, Saturday.	20 minutes before Booked Trains.	2.30 a.m. Monday.

Drivers of all other Trains, including Goods Trains, Cattle Trains, Light Engines, and Specials must be prepared to stop at each Level Crossing to open the gates.

No Special Trains must be run on these Branches during the time the line is closed (except as provided for below, without previous arrangement being made through the Junction Station Masters, or the District Inspector, who will arrange for the Station Masters along the Branch to be advised of the probable running time of the Special, and the Branch Station Masters must in turn advise the Crossing Gatekeepers under their charge.

Should, however, an emergency arise, rendering it necessary for a Special Train or Light Engine to be sent without such advice, the Driver must be prepared to stop at each level crossing, as the gates may be closed against the line.

Buckingham in mid-1920's. An 18" goods waits with a train of five six-wheelers for Banbury. Note L.N.W.R. up starter and all the company's lamps in situ.

Chapter Eight

Buckingham

When the first Duke of Buckingham successfully opposed the first survey of the London and Birmingham Railway, which was planned to take a course through Buckingham, he effectively altered the future of the town. Had the railway passed through, then Buckingham would have been the site of the large locomotive and carriage works that was eventually built at Wolverton, together with the industrial development that followed it. With hindsight one may find different opinions as to whether this could have been a blessing or not, one thing is sure, Buckingham is now isolated or preserved, depending on one's point of view. Subsequent events show that the nearby town of Aylesbury was only too ready to fill the breach and wasted little time in attaching itself to the new railway, this gave the town a commercial advantage over the former county town that it has never lost. Buckingham therefore remained, and is to this day a largely agrarian economy, with tiny winding streets and buildings that have never altered much since before the coming of the railway in 1850. A branch of the Grand Union Canal arrived at Buckingham in 1801.

The second Duke of Buckingham took a completely opposite point of view from that of his father, and saw the advantages that the new railway could offer, accepting some responsibility for the town's isolation. His Grace together with Sir Harry Verney of Claydon drew up the plans to fulfil this need and after the two separate companies had been joined in the name of the Buckinghamshire Railway, he became chairman. His place in the chair was very short lived however, for as a result of some financial difficulties the second Duke left for abroad in 1847. Family association with the line did not perish, as the Duke's son, the Marquess of Chandos, who was a keen railway enthusiast, was only too pleased to take his place on the board, whilst Sir Harry Verney filled the vacant chairmanship.

The Buckingham station that opened for business on 1st May, 1850 was a different affair to the more grand appearance on the photographs.

The original station was a menial wooden building opening onto the Lenborough Road (or Mount Pleasant side, opposite the subsequent entrance) and had very poor access, being virtually in the middle of a field, along a footpath. In 1853 the Marquess of Chandos had the Chandos Road cut through to the line from the town side whilst the corporation petitioned the railway company to build a new and sufficient station. This was the familiar structure of Doric, cornice and pediment designed by J.W. Livock and opened by 1861, by which time the population of Buckingham was just under 4,000. Further, the railway company also made a connecting road from the new Chandos Road to the Gawcott Road so that passengers from that side of the line could drive through to the new booking office; this was named Station Road, and after some lengthy contentions between the corporation and the Railway Company it was finally adopted by the borough in 1897. A local newspaper, the Buckingham Express described the station in its early days when "Ballast was so high as to conceal the wooden blocks or timbers and one signal post between the running line and the loop line was fixed with two arms, for running in both directions" and "A poster on the platform encouraged emigration to New York via Liverpool."

During the building of the line a contractor's locomotive named 'Trio' was brought by road from Wolverton, this was manhandled and coaxed through the narrow streets of the town which was thronged with sightseers and after practically demolishing the Tingewick Road Bridge and falling onto the line it was eventually installed into service. In 1857 the Castle Foundry which manufactured steam driven machinery was opened adjoining the station, in later years when the foundry ceased production its buildings were absorbed into the milk factory complex. In 1857 Sir Harry Verney became Member of Parliament for Buckingham for the second time. It was also a time for railway excursions, and they were proudly advertised in the local press. One such excursion that year left for Crystal Palace pulling out of Buckingham at 7.25 am and arriving at Euston at 9.30 am; the fares for the return trip were, First class 6s. 0d. (30p), covered carriages 4s. 0d. (20p).

To this same exhibition travelled 200 dozen Banbury cakes per week from a Buckingham Baker.

In this first exuberant decade all mail was brought direct to the town, foot carriers, horse riders and mail coaches soon became a thing of the past. A railway messenger was appointed at Buckingham to collect the mail from the station, and to deliver outgoing mail there. It is amusing to note that in 1851 the following minute was presented to the board, 'that the letter carrier and railway messenger at Buckingham be allowed the assistance of his son on the understanding that the department is put to no additional expense by the arrangement.'

The authorising act contained clauses about the rates to be charged for merchandise:

Commodity	Rate per ton per mile	In Railway Co's Wagons	Hauled by Co's Engines
Compost, lime, dung, manure, limestone,	1d. (½p)	plus ½d.	plus ½d.
Coals, coke, culm, charcoal.	1½d. (1p)	plus ½d.	plus 1d.
Sugar, grain, cotton, wool, manufactured goods	3d. (1½p)	plus 1d.	plus 2d. (1p)
Carriages under 1 ton.	6d. (2½p) each	plus 2d. each	plus 2d. each
Horses	3d. each	plus 1d. each	plus 1d. each
Calves	1d. each	plus ¼d. each	plus ¾d. each
Passengers	2d. each	plus ½d. each	plus ½d. each

In the agricultural depression of 1870's Buckingham was badly affected and this became apparent in the poor market days.

In 1879 the 'Buckingham Express' carried a letter of criticism from one of the patrons of the railway complaining of the bad connections between the Oxford and Banbury lines. The letter commented rather acidly, "Is this arrangement likely to save the Company the loss (of which the LNWR complained) of £20,000 per annum on the Banbury branch". This was by no means an isolated example of the comments that were being made at a time, not twelve months after the Buckinghamshire Railway had been totally absorbed by the LNWR.

In January 1881 the Buckingham Express reported that the town was completely isolated by snow, four engines from Bletchley being stuck at Verney Junction. The down 7 pm train from Banbury was stuck at Cockley Brake and hundreds of men were working continuously to try and open the line. All the shops and traders in the towns were required to close early in order to save gas. There were no trains for two days and the first one to complete its journey on the branch early on Thursday morning took three hours.

A month later there must have been a great change in the weather when the station became the centre of great festivity on welcoming the Duke of Buckingham's return from India, where he had been Governor of the Madras Presidency. By 1885 the station was *en fete* once more when the Duke returned from London and his wedding, leaving Euston at 2 pm and arriving at Buckingham in a single saloon carriage at 4.20 pm. Sadly the Duke was to remain only another four years before he died.

The palatial residence of Stowe was then let to the Comte de Paris, the royalist claimant to the French throne, this was in 1890. Whilst he was in residence the station nameboards were displayed bi-lingually as an aid to his staff when passing through the station. When he died in 1894 only part of Stowe was occupied by Lady Kinloss. In 1921 the great palace that had cost nearly £3,000,000 to build and furnish, was sold for £40,000, many of its documents being dispersed, a large number to America.

The year of 1898 seemed to herald happier days for this small town station when the Prince of Wales passed through en route for Stowe where he was to review the Royal Bucks. Hussars. The Branch began to build up to a brisk service and W.H. Smith installed one of their book-stalls on the platform, later a change of contract resulted in Smith's business being transferred into the town, their place was taken by Wymans. This was also the time when Buckingham justified a slip carriage detached at Bletchley from a northbound train each day. An excursion each Thursday to Euston allowed for a late return with a train from Euston leaving at 12.10 am and arriving at Buckingham at 1.50 am, quite a challenge for the White Hart Hotel in Buckingham which boasted . . . 'Every train is met'.

At the beginning of the twentieth century milk was becoming a developing source of trade in the area as the town had quite a large catchment area of dairy farms with all the local farmers having an account for sending milk to Watford or London by rail. To ensure that their produce would be upon the daily milk train there was many a wild ride of horse and cart through country lanes before rattling and screeching to a halt outside the station. So substantial was the milk traffic that it created the necessity for handling the product within the town itself, this became manifest by the construction of the milk factory that faced the station. Early names of this company were the Anglo-Swiss Condensed Milk Co. and Condensed and Peptonised Milk Co., later it was known as Thew, Hook and Gilbey and in its final years became a branch of the United Dairies. The factory processed milk for a number of products; some was despatched to Purfleet where Van den Burghs used it in margarine. A hundred 10 gallon churns were sent each day to 'Ovaltine' at Kings Langley, it was also turned into condensed milk, chocolate and malt. The factory's relationship with the railways continued to prosper well until the late forties when road transport was becoming much more competitive, even the LMS were not above sending a load of fresh cream by road when it was regarded as being more convenient to do so. For many years regular deliveries of coal were drawn across the road and into the United Dairies from the station. Today part of the building is still in use by that company for research but most of the large factory structure is now used for storing cement; a road depot for receiving milk exists in another part of the town.

In 1904 Mrs Rogers who was at that time the Mayoress of Bucking-ham, donated a horse trough to the station. This was useful not only for the dray and carrier horses but also for the 'trace' horse which was employed on light shunting duties around the station. Many of these duties were between the milk factory and the station and a mill along-side the factory which also had a siding, all evidence of which has long since disappeared. During those early days before the first world war a quaint old horse bus used to stand awaiting business outside the station. In common with all other country stations Buckingham would handle a large variety of produce beside the staple coal and milk; fruit and vegetables, mushrooms, blackberries, livestock and even maggots(!) were all carried by the railway. On one occasion a Mr Davies had his entire farm transported on one train all the way from Wales. Regular stops had to be made along the way to milk the cows and water the horses.

By the time of the outbreak of the first world war the LNWR had decided to make a number of economies on the branch, one of these was the closing of the small signalbox at Buckingham goods yard which was 750 yards north of the station. This section was the only double track length to be installed on the branch and as a result the down line was severed at the station and buffer stops were placed there. Some of the up side was then removed and a connection was re-made by slewing the track across the bridge, see diagram. The long siding was then used to store a mixture of stock passing from and to Wolverton. A home signal at Buckingham was some forty feet high and could be seen by enginemen above the Tingewick road bridge near the goods yard. The wartime construction of the ammunition works at Banbury intensified goods train working through Buckingham and provided employment for many of the young women who lived there and travelled daily into Banbury.

Just after the war there was an incident that nearly got signalman Harris and porter Bert Williams the sack. A favourite pastime of some Buckingham youths was to venture up to the station unseen and enter one of the vans parked on the siding next to the cattle landing, their delight used to be to release the brake and sit on the wheel-shaped handle to spin round. On one such occasion the van must have been a particularly free-running one as it began to move on release and roll down to the running line where, upon reaching the throw-off point it toppled over, straddling the line. Fortunately an approaching train was still some distance away, fortunate too for the two railwaymen who had the guilt aimed in their direction. At a resulting enquiry the station-master was able to give evidence that he had witnessed the badly shaken youth climbing out of the van and running away, so the two men were absolved.

On the subject of station staff it is interesting to list the requirements of a station of Buckingham's size in the late LNWR days. The payroll was as follows: Station Master; 2 Passenger Clerks; 3 Goods Clerks;

Buckingham station garden in the 1920's — very L.N.W.R. In later years the ½ mile post was moved back, higher on the slope. Note the all-

2 Signalmen; 2 Porters (one of these would be a relief signalman); 1 Goods Shunter; and boy assistant; 1 dray (eventually lorry) driver; 4 Platelayers.

Porter and later relief signalman for the branch Bert Williams joined the LNWR at Buckingham on leaving the army at the end of the first world war, this was in the year of 1919. He still resides in one of those narrow Buckingham streets, a lively character with a bright eye and a sharp memory and although he has now turned the age of seventy he paddles backward and forward to his allotment by boat! Bert has always been keen to occupy his leisure time with some form of horticulture and it was not long after he took his position at the station that he rented an orchard, to this he added a smallholding of pigs and a fowl run, which he has continued to maintain to this day. During the second world war pig food was severely rationed, but it was more easily available to any unified body. Bert immediately founded a Pig Club amongst the local keepers and greatly eased a serious problem. Not to rest upon his laurels Bert also set about the task, along with other railwaymen, of forming the Buckingham (Railway Section) of the Home Guard, the obvious requirement being to mount a unit for the protection of the line.

Originally facilities for loading and unloading cattle were provided at the goods yard, but government legislation during the 1930's enforced the requirement that water should be available for cattle when loading and unloading and as a result the landing was brought to the station and was installed on the site of the original station platform. On one occasion a herd of cattle ran amok when the landing was in the goods yard and ran down the line in the direction of Brackley where they came into contact with the 5 pm train from Brackley; this killed four and injured several others so that they had to be destroyed by a vet. In the early 1920's an oil depot was installed at the goods yard, the first tentative steps of that unit which has survived the railway with an elaborate structure today. All coal deliveries went to the goods yard and a large timber structure has been added alongside the goods shed to handle what appears to have been some very large deliveries, there are still many houses in the area using open fires for heating.

In 1923 Stowe School was founded and from then on each term would see the hoards of pupils descend on the station. The station staff would then shunt the extraordinary ten coach trains with their exuberant cargo often spilling itself into the "sixfoot" and scrambling all over the running lines. A traditional goodbye from some of the boys would be to catapult the station clock.

Buckingham station gardens had always been a source of pride to the staff but the competitive side received a real impetus when Bert Williams was joined by signalman Harold Plant. Together the two men set about attaining great heights in the heavily competitive world of station flower, fruit and vegetable competitions and during the 1930's the station of Buckingham represented the LMS (southern section — Euston to Northampton) against the stations of other railways at the London Horticulturist Society Show in London, and occasionally triumphed. Never complacent, the staff continued to compete in the southern section of the best kept station and garden award, the trophy being in the form of a shield. Not surprisingly they had several successes in this competition, one can well imagine the grimy branch goods standing amidst this blaze of floreat colour. One successful year was that of the Coronation of Her Majesty Queen Elizabeth II, this was the year of the *pièce de resistance* with a splendid flower arrangement of the royal motif surmounted by a silver crown. There were mixed fortunes for Harold and Ron Brookes (porter) when, after the judging had taken place the sky opened and released a torrential downpour, thus was their enterprise sodden and beaten flat, alas to rise no more. (The mitigating factor being that they had again won the shield outright.) Bert Williams left the station and went to work at the nearby United Dairies, in 1945.

Harold Plant and Ron Brookes pose with the prize-winning shield in 1953. Note the small greenhouse behind station building (down side) and another use for those steps!

Harold Plant

Harold Plant at the Buckingham box in the early 1950's. The L.M.S. cabin
replaced the L.N.W.R. when the latter was destroyed by fire in the winter of
1930-31. The Webb lever frame survived within the new cabin until closure. The
old cabin still had 'Buckingham No. 1' on the front, a distinction remaining from
the days of No. 2 box at the goods yard.

Harold Plant

By the late 1940's Sunday passenger trains were withdrawn and there
were only four each way on weekdays, it was obvious that the passenger
service was in difficulties. The coming of the motor vehicles had led to
a decline in railway traffic between the two wars, which was interrupted
by the second war when the railway was extended to the full once more.
After the end of petrol rationing the competition returned with greater
impact and closure of the line was talked of in the mid-1950's, when
after the ASLEF strike of 1955 much of the milk traffic was lost.
Reprieve took the form of the railcar experiment when the passenger
service was given a new lease of life.

In 1960 when the section from Buckingham to Banbury was closed,
Buckingham became the terminus for the branch passenger traffic. The
Stationmaster at that time was Mr Whitney who had left Brackley in
1955. On his retirement in 1962 he was replaced by a Mr Rodney S.
Hampson who took a keen interest in all railway business and I am glad
to say still does. I am indebted to him for this chronicle of events that
were in fact in the final days of Buckingham Station.

Buckingham at the time of closure of the Banbury extension.

Len's of Sutton

"In January 1963 when I recorded a temperature at the station of 10 degrees Fahrenheit the branch became blocked by drifts of snow from the 19th until being ploughed through to Banbury on the 30th. During this period it had just been possible to bring in trains of badly needed heating oil, often on a Sunday. The road to Winslow had been just as badly affected as the railway. One very clear example of the conditions at that time was when the trip engine went down the line to take water to Mrs Faulkner at the desolate spot of Bacon's House Crossing, and didn't return for two hours. By telephoning Brackley Central we got news that the engine was to be seen beyond Bacon's House, near where the Great Central line crossed the Banbury branch. When the engine did finally return the crew were somewhat vague about their long absence. What transpired was that they had tried to see how far along the line they could get and became stuck in a drift, east of the Great Central crossing bridge. I later saw a tremendous 'burn' on the rails at that point where the engine wheels had spun in the futile attempts to wrench itself free.

The first date that we heard for a discontinuing of passenger traffic was on the 7th of September, 1963 but this was deferred, subject to objections voiced at a public hearing in the following October. The line from Buckingham to Banbury closed to goods traffic on the 30th November, 1963. In the February of the following year a branch of Woolworths opened in Buckingham and as this company had a policy of moving their goods by rail we filled the old yard with vans full of the new merchandise. In that same month we started stabling condemned

coal wagons on the defunct section of the branch. As a result of this a
Westbury farmer made plain words of his objection to having his farm
crossing blocked by old railway wagons. This gave us the back-breaking
job of crowbarring a space between them, engine power being unavail-
able. On the 12th July, 1964 some wit sold the furthest wagons first
which gave the engine the task of drawing out 191 wagons to reach
them, costing the company £100 extra — what price blood, sweat and
tears at Westbury? In August we learned that the Verney Junction —
Buckingham section was to close for passengers on the 5th of
September. On the second of September condemned coaches began to
be placed on the branch where the now sold coal wagons had stood.
Inevitably the final day arrived, the words that I wrote down afterwards
were: 'I have just lost my first ship — she went down with colours flying
and in a cloud of smoke on Saturday night. There was quite a crowd on
the last train, but they were all railway enthusiasts, not local people.
Just a few locals and railway families turned up to hear all the detonators
go off — even the reporter only turned up the following Wednesday. Still,
we did our best — we gave the driver and guard each a bunch of flowers
from the station garden'.

No. 84002 on the auto-train at Buckingham. In the early fifties this train would
work through to Banbury; with the advent of the two railcars it would work in
conjunction between Bletchley and Buckingham.

Mr. J. Arrow

Buckingham Goods Yard and Refuge Siding.—The points leading from the single line to the Goods Yard and the Refuge Siding are controlled by the Electric Staff.

When it is necessary for a Train or Engine to be shunted into the Goods Yard or Refuge Siding and for the Staff to be taken back to Buckingham Signal Box to allow another train to pass, the following arrangements must be carried out :—

Between 8.15 p.m. and 7.45 a.m., the Signalman on Duty is responsible for working the Points, and after seeing that the whole of the Train is clear of the Main Line, closing and locking the Points and returning with the Staff to the Signal Box.

When the Train or Engine is ready to leave the Sidings, the signalman will take the Staff from the Signal Box and unlock the Points. After the Train or Engine has run out on to the Main Line and is ready to go right away, he will close and lock the Points and hand the Staff to the Driver in the usual way.

Between 7.45 a.m. and 8.15 p.m. the Guard will be responsible for working the Points and seeing that the Main Line is clear.

Drivers are authorised, between 7.45 a.m. and 8.15 p.m., after they have satisfied themselves that the Main Line is clear, to hand the Staff to the Platform Porter, who will at once walk back to Buckingham Signal Box and hand it to the Signalman.

When the train or engine is ready to leave the Sidings, a Staff will be handed to the Platform Porter to give to the Driver. (10/20)

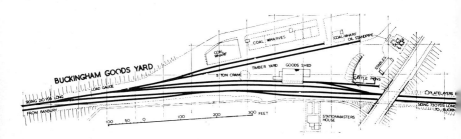

Buckingham goods yard as it appeared at the time of the grouping, in later years a smaller coal wharf landing was built adjoining the Buckingham side of the goods shed. The oil storage complex expanded onto the former site and remains so to the present day.

Railway Modeller

BUCKINGHAM.

Goods Yard and Refuge Siding.—When it is necessary for a train to be shunted into the goods yard or refuge siding to allow another train to pass, the signalman must work the points between 8.15 p.m. and 7.45 a.m., and the guard between 7.45 a.m. and 8.15 p.m.

Buckingham reference in Working Appendix March, 1937.

Working Appendix L.M.S. 1937, sidings worked under special arrangements.

L.M.S. — Cyril Gibbons

Sidings connected with running lines and which are worked under special arrangements—continued.		
Siding.	Position.	Particulars of working.
N. Yard	Farthinghoe	Ground frame, controlled by electric token.
Yard	Brackley	Ground frame, Annett's key from signal box.
N. Yard	Fulwell and Westbury	Ground frame, controlled by electric token.
N. Bacon's House	Fulwell and Westbury and Buckingham	,, ,, ,,
N. Station	Padbury	,, ,, ,,
Goods station	Buckingham...	,, ,, ,,
Down refuge		
N. Gough's		

This view of the old milk factory, which is now used for storing cement, was taken on the site of the razed station buildings.

Brian Garland

The old Buckingham goods yard stables being used for modern haulage — 1975.

Brian Garland

On the following Wednesday I noted that there were two miles of railway coaches on the branch — about 180 coaches. We nearly had an episode like the one with the coal wagons when an enquiry was made for a brake second as a carpet exhibition coach which was at that time standing next but one to Bacon's House Crossing. My suggestion of removing it from the Banbury end was not accepted!

Rostering of engines for goods working up the branch was extremely erratic even to the extent of a monster class 9F prowling into the station.

On the 9th February, 1966 we learnt that the branch was to close completely on the 11th March, 1966, excepting the Queen's visit, scheduled for the 4th April.

On the 3rd April at 10.30 pm the Queen left Windsor and the train came onto the branch in the early hours of the 4th at 1 am. It was headed by two diesel engines and banked at the rear with a third diesel and a train heating van. A recent failure in Norfolk by a diesel hauling a Royal train made the Railways Board nervous, thus the superpower; the rear engine was to haul off the heating van, should it prove faulty — it did! The villagers of Padbury had a pleasant surprise when they awoke on the following morning to find the Royal train in their station. I went to Padbury when it was stabled, and had various doings with police and GPO men — they installed two phone lines on the train and another in Padbury station building, for police use. I then went home for a brief sleep, only to be up early on the following morning to collect the newspapers from W.H. Smiths in Buckingham and take them to the Royal Train."

At Buckingham there had been some rather hurried restoration and spring cleaning which was touchingly nostalgic, harkening back to those earlier and more graceful Victorian and Edwardian days of travel. Returned to former grace the old station could for one brief shining moment forget that this was in fact its swan song. At ten o'clock the Royal train drew alongside the platform and the Superintendent who travelled on the train introduced Mr Hampson to Her Majesty and HRH the Duke of Edinburgh who, after remarking upon the shallowness of the platform was informed by the Superintendent that as the station was a very old one it could possibly be sinking! I daresay such a spectacular explanation would have invited an interesting reply from the Duke. A red carpet ran from the platform edge and out through the portacle, upon this was placed a specially constructed set of steps — someone had remembered Brackley!

Mr Hampson was made redundant and left the railway in 1966, this does not appear to have impaired his enthusiasm for the topic as he still gives talks and writes excellent historical accounts with accomplished skill.

Buckingham goods was officially open until January, 1967 when it too was also closed, by the stroke of a pen. Twelve months later the

Buckingham goods shed on the side where rails are no more.

Brian Garland

A view of Buckingham goods shed interior with simple 'gallows' crane on platform with central pivot affixed to roof truss.

Brian Garland

rails that had so recently held the Royal train were removed and the last employee on the Banbury branch — Harold Plant, locked his box for the last time. For Buckingham the age of the iron horse had passed, passenger transport to and from the towns and villages now being provided by a Midland Red omnibus service. The station buildings have now been completely demolished and the yew hedge donated by Lord Addington remains but is wildly overgrown. The two empty bridges are supporting nothing more than grass, earth and cinders where one may take a quiet evening stroll to appreciate the high level view of this small but fascinating Buckinghamshire town.

R.S. Hampson concluded his reminiscences with a simplified diagram of the frequency of passenger trains throughout the life of the branch and the receipts of passenger traffic during the last full year of trains between Bletchley and Buckingham.

Year	Weekdays		Sundays	
	Up	Down	Up	Down
1857	4	4	1	1
1869	5	5	1	1
1887	5	5	2	2
1911	6	6	1	1
1942	4	4	1	1
1959	9	9	-	-
1964	8	8	-	-

In the last full year there were 6,600 passengers, with receipts of £4,000. This included 1,000 @ £1,250 carried on Stowe School specials, so that the remaining 5,600 passengers and £2,750 receipts averaged two per train, £1 receipts — no wonder that United Counties wouldn't run a one-man bus service in substitution at closure!

Buckingham end loading dock for wheeled transport.

Brian Garland

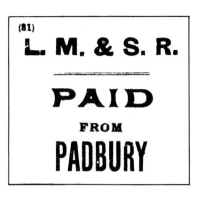

Chapter Nine

Padbury

The village of Padbury is just under four miles from Buckingham and two and a quarter miles from Verney Junction. The railway station had a single platform with a brick building and one siding, in the manner of Farthinghoe, but unlike Farthinghoe it was closely convenient to the village that it served. Padbury was not opened for service until 1st March, 1878, shortly after Fulwell and Westbury. There does not however appear to be any station master's house, in all probability the few men there to occupy this position at Padbury lived in one of the houses close by, as Mr Haslop did at Banbury. It is recorded that the opening took place on a damp and uncomfortable day, but that the new station was neatly encircled with evergreens. A villager remarked that "the station is a great boon and will enable people from Buckingham to attend concert next Monday". The concert had been arranged by the choir to raise funds for a new school clock and the fare for each of those attending from Buckingham would be 2½d. (1p) single and 6d. (2½p) first class single.

During the year of 1909 there occurred what was one of the most dramatic incidents to take place on the line. In the month of April in that year a terrible accident was averted by the heroism of a goods guard, one Jim Bates. The saga was like something out of a silent film of that time, but in his case it was all too frighteningly real. The episode was well chronicled in a newspaper report of that time under the heading — 'Bletchley Guard's Heroism': "The engine of the goods train, composed of about a dozen trucks, loaded with coal, granite, etc., which had been shunting on the siding at Padbury station, appears to have been left unattended for a few seconds, (amazingly the driver jumped off to pick violets whilst the fireman jumped off in the same moment to answer the call of nature, it is noted that the two men seldom conversed) and in some unexplained manner started off down the line.

L. M. & S. R.   PADBURY

RATING PLAN

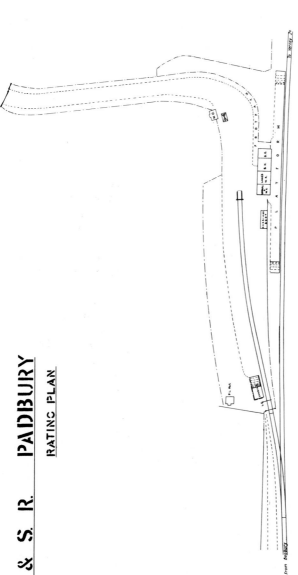

Scale 40 Feet to 1 Inch

Padbury ground plan of station, early 1930's. So little ever altered at Padbury throughout its long life that it could be regarded as almost any-
time. The 'Carriage Body' referred to is in fact an old L.N.W.R. goods van.

Padbury the country station. This view, looking towards Verney, was taken at the time of the grouping (1923). The hatless gentleman is quite the exception, as the Guard patiently waits for the woman who is saying some farewells. A pleasant rustic scene taken from the moment of one of those long summer evenings many years ago.

Mr. D. Thompson

Bates in his brake-van, realised in a flash that after the train had run through Buckingham on the single line it would reach Westbury, where a passenger train from Banbury would be standing. He crawled from his van to the last of the dozen trucks which made up the goods train, and, hanging over the side of it, reached down and loosed the long lever that put the brake on. Then he crawled to the next truck, and did the same thing, and then to the next. It was a most perilous task, for the trucks were filled with granite and coal. Meanwhile the train had dashed through Buckingham station at a great speed, to the consternation of the officials, who seeing that there was no one on the engine telegraphed to the next station. Although the footplate was untenanted by driver or fireman, the officials could plainly discern the guard crawling from truck to truck and dropping the brakes.

Bates also tried to reach the engine, but the space between the leading truck and the locomotive was so great as to make this impossible. His work however had told. The engine could not pull the dozen heavy trucks with their brakes on. Presently he was encouraged by the slackening speed, and just outside Westbury station the runaway train came to a standstill.

It was now on a single line, and in front stood the passenger train from Banbury and Brackley. But for the coolness and pluck shown by Bates an awful catastrophe must have resulted. The goods train was brought back to Buckingham, where the breathless driver and stoker had already arrived, having run the two and a quarter miles from Padbury.

123

Padbury in the last decade looking toward Buckingham, the steps remain in place for the railcar whilst the weeds slowly advance from behind the fencing. Note L.N.W.R. seat with name recessed in support.

Len's of Sutton

Padbury in final years looking toward Verney. Note van behind nameboard and the shortened chimney stacks, a common occurrence with these ageing stations.

Len's of Sutton

They feared a disaster, and were much relieved to find that no damage had been done".

Bates listened to all the praise for his 'sharp exciting run' with great reserve and self-effacing modesty, he claimed to have done no more than his duty. He was a resolute workman of forty-five years of age, seventeen of them with the railway company which he joined in 1882. His reward came later in the form of promotion to Station Master. The two footplate men were summarily dismissed, the chairman of the company, Sir Guy Calthorpe did not take too kindly to the fact that the first news of the matter came to him via the press.

At the time of this episode the Station Master at Padbury was a man who became the line's centenarian, Levi Ambler, who worked with his son Fred as Porter. Levi Ambler, like Henry Somerton served nearly all of his working life on the branch, aspiring first of all to signalman at Buckingham and then moving for promotion to Padbury where he remained until his retirement in 1928. He died in Winslow at the age of 100 years in 1967. After his retirement the position of Station Master was not maintained at Padbury leaving the requirement of one Porter and junior assistant, instructed by the Station Master at Buckingham.

When the station was opened the population of Padbury was 661 persons, it is now 466 persons. Being a moderately sized village without any significant form of industry the population like so many other villages in the area, depended largely upon the farming community for their livelihood. The arrival of the railway encouraged people to travel further for their employment than hitherto, and was made considerable use of by this village in particular. The sidings were controlled by the familiar ground frame released by electric token and would often accommodate the usual four or five wagons of coal per week, plus manifold requirements of the community. Appreciable amounts of milk were despatched from there to the United Dairies factory at Buckingham.

The heavy days of 1942 took a lighthearted turn at Padbury, when the responsibility of the station fell upon the shoulders of a single porter, Mrs Allen. Mrs Allen was employed by the LMS as a temporary wartime expedient that continued for a further twenty-four years, completed when the station was closed for passengers on the 7th September, 1964, nine months later than its closure for goods, thus were the people of Padbury loath to lose their railway. Mrs Allen's years of devotion to railway service did not prevent her from bringing up six healthy and happy children against a background that most children would envy. Very often they would assist her in carrying out some of the station tasks and knew all the Bletchley enginemen that travelled the line, one of the boys 'Darby' Allen would occasionally get on the footplate and 'have a go', one engine he remembered having this exciting experience on was No. 44447. One can imagine that the life at the little country station could not have been too dissimilar to E.R. Nesbitt's story of the 'Railway Children', developing romantic

No. 84002 makes its only branch line call at Padbury with the solitary figure of Mrs Allan in attendance. A fresh poster on the station notice board loudly exclaims 'Now! diesel trains between BUCKINGHAM and BANBURY', whilst the charm of Padbury is totally unmoved, and is captured superbly in this photograph.
W.A. Camwell

Mrs Allan with three of her children in 1942. The daughter, Hilda later took up a post at Buckingham station. The other two boys are Bill and eldest brother Sid. Note the wartime posters and the use of old sleepers, on which they are standing.

Mr. D. Allan

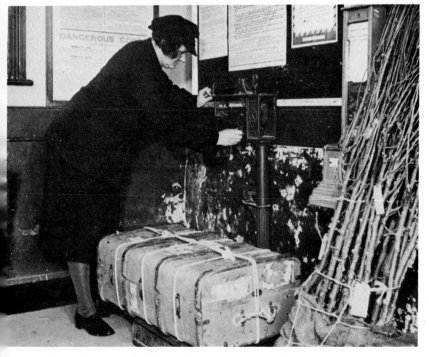

A variety of merchandise, Mrs Allan weighs the goods. Note the 'One Penny' chocolate bar machine behind the consignment of trees.

Mr. D. Allan

Inside the station Mrs Allan uses the antique telephone. Fresh flowers in a jam jar add a pleasant touch to the rather spartan setting.

Mr. D. Allan

A tired looking 'Cauliflower' rumbles into Padbury in 1942.

Mr. D. Allan

Mrs Allan takes down the wagon numbers, to be phoned through to Bletchley (1942).

Mr. D. Allan

Another use for those steps as Mrs Allan pastes up the new wartime posters using 'an 'orrible glue'. The small railway poster above the Red Cross and St. John appeal strictures travellers on the harmful and inconvenient habit of smoking on their trains.

associations when one of Mrs Allen's daughters married one of the firemen on the line, a Mr Judge.

Unfortunately government policy is not peculiar to the local needs but rather more to larger considerations, and the little station at Padbury closed despite the angry fusillades of posters and petitions of its locals. How Mrs Allen must have felt when her sons waved as they rode on the last train can only be conjectured, after 24 years of running the station single handed.

The station buildings were finally demolished in 1968 and the ground cleared. By 1975 a new housing development was under way and the site of the line was totally obliterated, again, in the manner of Farthinghoe.

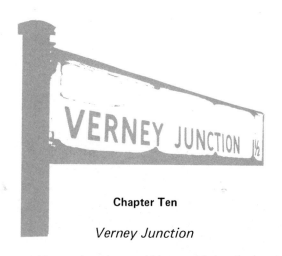

Chapter Ten

Verney Junction

In some ways Verney Junction could be regarded as the heart of the Buckinghamshire Railway. It took its name from that esteemed promoter of the lines Sir Harry Verney whose home, Claydon is situated nearby; apart from the tenants of the estate and their cluster of cottages there is little in the way of any village or township. Its main role has been as an interchange station to other routes, especially for goods traffic. It was not considered necessary at all until that contentious connection with Aylesbury was made by the Aylesbury and Buckingham Railway in September, 1868. The LNWR viewed the Aylesbury and Buckingham Railway's progress with extreme disfavour and constructed the station and every detail at the smaller companies cost. Sir Harry Verney who was on the board of the A&B which was chaired by the Duke of Buckingham and heavily invested in by both of them, must have been rancoured by the LNWR's obstructive attitude, especially when Sir Harry had already done so much to promote the earlier lines, and had from the outset endeavoured to see the two towns of Aylesbury and Buckingham on a direct rail link, continuing north and south.

Thus by 1868 Verney Junction in its most rudimentary form was opened to passenger traffic, but when the A&B advertised connections to and from Banbury, Oxford and Bletchley the LNWR adopted a hostile attitude, and encouraged its passengers to use the circuitous route to Aylesbury via Bletchley and Cheddington. Finding themselves isolated by the LNWR, the A&B looked to the GWR to run their line from the joint station at Aylesbury. This the Great Western agreed to do and so for nearly twenty years the Swindon motif was face to face with that of Crewe, until the Metropolitan Railway, absorbed the parlous A&B and made Verney Junction their northern terminus on 1st July, 1891.

If one were to read any biographical account of that famous reformer, Florence Nightingale, one would soon come across the name

Verney Junction in the twenties, the station looking traditionally neat with a fine array of Metropolitan coaches in the old A. & B. platform.

Len's of Sutton

Verney Junction in early 1930's. A distant mineral train behind a G2 is held at the home whilst the 18" goods brings in a train from Banbury. Good display of period signs on the right.

Mr. D. Thompson

18" Goods No. 8367 in charge of a three coach train, pauses at Verney c. 1930.

Photomatic

of Verney and the house at Claydon. Sir Harry Verney was considered by both his tenants and constituents to be a generous and considerate man who made great efforts to improve the living standards of the poor. During the cholera epidemic of 1844 he worked diligently amongst the sick and later collected funds to build the country hospital at Aylesbury. It is therefore not surprising that he should form a lasting friendship with this great lady of her time, for whom he had a deep admiration. This friendship prospered over the years and Florence Nightingale made many journeys from London to Claydon, which she considered to be her second home, residing there for quite long periods.

In 1893, at the age of 93, Sir Harry Verney died. He had led a fruitful and active life in the county of Buckinghamshire, developing its resources and bequeathing many valuable institutions to its population, not least of which was the opportunity to travel. This legacy remained over a hundred years until a time when the whole concept of public transport had vastly altered; the railway served them well.

After the A&B was absorbed by the Metropolitan it was elevated to main line status when the Manchester, Sheffield and Lincolnshire Railway (later Great Central Railway) opened its extension to London. At about the same time a service of through trains between Baker Street and Verney Junction was inaugurated, although this facility can hardly have been economically justified.

One of the familiar L.N.W.R. steam railcars at Bicester in 1903. Time tables record this vehicle running into Buckingham but there is no evidence to affirm that it ever ran beyond that station.

Brian Garland

When the Metropolitan Railway decided to close down the Aylesbury to Verney section in 1936 the link with Buckingham was finally severed, on the other hand it is unlikely to have been closed had it shown any kind of return, as railway owners had not by then reached the age of asphyxiating their offsprings. Nevertheless during its short life time, by railway standards, there had been an interesting connection from this tiny rustic community into the huge capital, and it had seen the regular use of two Pullman cars named 'Mayflower' and 'Galatea' in 1910.

In 1939 a start was made to remove one of the tracks of this line, and this work was completed on 28th January, 1940. The remaining single line carried some wartime traffic, but was completely closed soon after the war, before the actual rails were removed it was used for coach and wagon storage.

Thus by the last thirty years of the Banbury branch we see the Verney Junction station severed from its purpose, as far as passenger traffic was concerned, and it is difficult to see of what further use it could be save for the interchange of local services. The transfer of goods between the lines was still a useful requirement, but I am sure that most passengers visiting Oxford or Banbury could route themselves by more convenient alternatives.

Verney Junction near the time of closure. The down starter signals of the L.N.W.R. have been replaced by a new bracket with a lattice post and the field behind it has acquired a pylon. The indomitable L.N.W.R. station nameboard with its proclamation of exchange train facilities has yielded to the utilitarian and parsimonious requirement of British Railways, in concrete and maroon enamel. A station garden that is novel and brave appears to have lost heart; in its midst a derelict lamp seems to say it all.

Len's of Sutton

A view taken from the other direction has little to distinguish it from any other run-down station, perhaps the platform needs mowing.

Len's of Sutton

Booking Office now serves as a wood shed and utility store for farm materials.
Brian Garland

Stationmaster's House retains an air of moderate prosperity next to the ruined station, the smaller building to the rear is the booking office. Note the date on the stone lintel inside apex of porch. 'Victoria 1870'.

Brian Garland

Verney Junction closed to passenger traffic on New Year's Day 1968, closing for goods some twelve months later. Today pigeons fly in and out of the modest booking hall, the station master's house is privately occupied, the letterbox built into its wall still carries the Royal motif, 'VR'. There are no station buildings left on the platforms, nor any trace of the lattice overbridge, whilst the rails that carry the freight trains hauled by bronchial diesels with their pungent black breath and loud klaxon warnings, do so between two crumbling platforms of grass. The trackbed of the Banbury branch has now become a moss and cinder road trailing into the obscurity of the Buckinghamshire countryside, much favoured by rabbits. Many of the mileposts remain as do bridges, culverts and wooden crossing gates and for anyone who loves the countryside it is a very pleasant walk. For railway enthusiasts it has become one of many such lines that are slowly disappearing beneath the surrounding fields, the last vestiges of a pace and refinement belonging to another age.

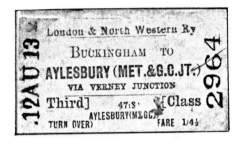

BLOCK SECTIONS OF THE BANBURY BRANCH

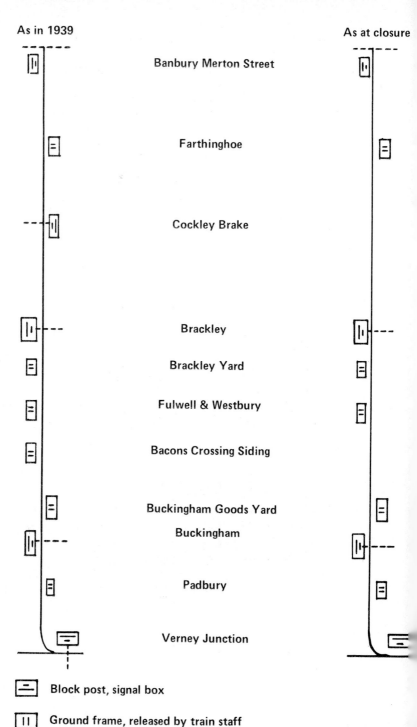

As in 1939   As at closure

Banbury Merton Street

Farthinghoe

Cockley Brake

Brackley

Brackley Yard

Fulwell & Westbury

Bacons Crossing Siding

Buckingham Goods Yard

Buckingham

Padbury

Verney Junction

Block post, signal box

Ground frame, released by train staff

Block sections of the branch.   A.N. Emmerson

Electric Staff Apparatus.	... / 4	... / 862	Verney Junction — Buckingham (Passenger Station)	... / ...	*Week-days.*—After the "Train out of Section" Signal has been received for the 7.15 p.m. Goods from Banbury until 5.20 a.m. *Sundays.*—Is only open for the passage of booked trains.
	7	519	Brackley Station ...	...	*Week-days.*—After the "Train out of Section" has been received for the 7.15 p.m. Goods from Banbury till 5.30 a.m. *Sundays.*—Is open only for the passage of booked trains.
	4	171	Cockley Brake Jn. ...	...	*Week-days.*—After "Train out of Section" Signal has been received for the 6.58 p.m. Passenger from Bletchley until 5.45 a.m. *Sundays.*—Is open only for the passage of booked trains.
	5	592	Banbury Station ...	...	*Week-days.*—After disposal of the 6.58 p.m. Passenger Train from Bletchley until 5.50 a.m. *Week-ends.*—After disposal of the 6.58 p.m. Passenger Train from Bletchley Saturday until 8.10 p.m. Sunday, and from 8.45 p.m. Sunday to 5.50 a.m. Monday.

Working time-table 1922 (opening and closing times of signal boxes).

J. Lowe

LIST OF SINGLE LINES OF RAILWAY.

Single lines of Railway worked on the Electric Token Block System.

Notes—T......Electric Train Tablet.
S......Electric Train Staff.
KT...Key Token.

Section of line.	Whether electric tablet, staff, etc.	Shape of token.	Colour of token.	Token stations.	Persons appointed to receive token from, and deliver it to, the driver.
Banbury Branch ...	S	Special miniature	Blue	Banbury	,,
,,	S	,, ...	Red	Cockley Brake Junction	,,
,,	S	,, ...	Blue	Brackley	,,
,,	S	,, ...	Red ...	Buckingham	Signalman; also station master or porter between 7.45 a.m. and 8.15 p.m.
				Verney Junction ...	Signalman

Working Appendix details on electric train staff 1937.

Cyril Gibbons

Electric shunting horns, gongs, or bells are provided at the following places for the purpose of signalling to drivers engaged in shunting operations—continued.

Place.	Line to which horn, gong or bell applies.	Remarks.
Willesden South West sidings ...	Up goods to sidings	Mechanical gong. Lever on back road, south west sidings.
Camden Down side	Down goods	Mechanical gong. Lever on South side of Camden No. 2 signal box.
Euston Down side shed	Nos. 1 and 2 shunting necks ...	Mechanical gong. Lever near No. 4 signal box, between shunting neck and retaining wall.
Long Buckby	Up	Mechanical gong. Worked from signal box.
Northampton No. 4	Up side shunting neck	Mechanical gong. Lever near north end shunter's hut.
Northampton	New down sidings hump ...	Klaxon horn. Plunger on electric light standard near shunter's hut.
Verney Junction	Down Oxford	Mechanical gong. Worked from signal box.
Acton, Old Oak Junction ...	Nos. 1 and 2 down loops ...	Mechanical gong. Lever near Old Oak up main home signal. Guards and shunters must see that the points are

Section from Working Appendix refers to the mechanical gong at Verney.

OXFORD, BANBURY

WEEKDAYS.

Miles	Miles	For continuation of trains from junctions, see page	Classification			1	2	3	4	5	6	7	8	9	10	11	12	13
						C	B	B	B	B	B	B	C		B	B	B	B
						PARCELS 3.0 a.m., Marylebone to Crewe					MIXED to Bilsworth.	To Cambridge.	Empty Stock to Bicester C.O.D. Exchange Sidings.		To Oxford		To Cambridge.	
						MX							SO		SO			
						a.m.	a.m.	a.m.	a.m.	a.m.	a.m.	a.m.	a.m.		a.m.	p.m.	p.m.	p.m.
0			OXFORD	dep.	1	....	6 25	6 45	....	8 0	....	10 15	10 50	....	....	....	2 42	....
5¾			Islip	arr.	2	Rep. No. 459.	6 35	6 55	..	..	..	10 25	..	..	..	..	..	..
				dep.	3		6 36	6 56		....	....	10 26	....	....	....	....	2 52	....
11¾			Bicester	arr.	4		6 45	7 6	N—Arr. 7.40.	8 18	..	10 35	11†10	..	11 50	..	3 1	..
				dep.	5		6 46	7 9		8 19	....	10 37		....	....	....	3 3	....
14			Launton	arr.	6		6 51	..		..	..	..	†—No. 2.	..	..	..	..	..
				dep.	7	....	6 52	....	....	....	....	....		....	....	....	3 8	....
16¼			Marsh Gibbon & Poundon	..	8	..	6 57	..	..	8 27	..	10 45		..	..	..	3 13	..
20			Claydon		9	4L45§	7 5	....	....	8 35	....	10 53		....	....	....	3 21	....
	0		BANBURY ⊕	dep.	10	..	..	..	7 15	..	10 40	..	..	..	..	1 40	..	3 4
	3¾		Farthinghoe		11	§—L.N.E. Jn. and arrives 4L20 a.m.	....	....	....	....	10 49	....	....	....	C.O.D. Exchange Sidings dep. 11.45 a.m.	1 48	....	3 5
	5¼		Cockley Brake Jn. ⊕	..	12		..	..	7*26	..	10*53	..	..	..		1*52	..	3*5
	9¼		Brackley ⊕	arr.	13		†—P.B. 7.31.	....	7 33	....	....	....	....	....		....	....	4
				dep.	14			..	7 34	..	..	..	..	..		1 59	..	4
	12¼		Fulwell & Westbury		15			....	7N41	....	....	....	....	....		2 5	....	4
	16¾		Buckingham ⊕	arr.	16			..	7 49	..	..	..	..	..		2 13	..	4 1
				dep.	17	....		....	7 50	....	....	....	....	....		2 17	....	4
	19		Padbury .. (H)		18	..	..	..	7 55	..	..	..	..	..	..	2 22	..	4
21¾	21¼		Verney Junction ⊕	arr.	19	....	7 9	7 26	8 0	....	....	....	....	....	Not advertised.	....	3 25	4
				dep.	20	4 51	7 10	7 27	8 1	8 39	..	10 57	..	..		2 27	3 26	4
24			Winslow	arr.	21	....	7 15	7 32	8 6	8 43	....	11 1	....	....		2 32	3 31	4
				dep.	22	..	7 16	..	8 8	8 44	..	11 3	..	..		2 33	3 32	4
25¾			Swanbourne		23	....	7 21	....	8 13	8 49	....	11 8	....	....		2 37	3 37	4
31¼		424	BLETCHLEY	arr.	24	5 7	7†30	..	8 22	8 58	..	11 17	..	..	..	2 46	3 46	4

H—Worked as a Halt for 7.0 p.m. Banbury to Bletchley.

BLETCHLEY, BANBURY

WEEKDAYS.

Miles	Miles	Classification			1	2	3	4	5	6	7	8	9	10	11	12	13	14
					C	C	B	B	B	B	B	C	B	B	B	B		B
					Empty Stock (vans) to High Wycombe.	PARCELS					9.16 a.m. from Bilsworth.	Empty Stock 10.50 a.m. from Oxford.	11.45 a.m. from Bicester C.O.D. Exchange Sidings.					
					MX							SO	SO					
					a.m.	a.m.	a.m.	a.m.	a.m.	a.m.	a.m.	a.m.	noon	p.m.	p.m.	p.m.		p.
0		BLETCHLEY	dep.	1	3 45	4 30	5 24	....	8 0	9 30	....	....	....	12 15	1 34	2 22	....	5
5¼		Swanbourne	..	2	3L55§	..	5T35	..	8 11	9 41	..	..	..	12 26	1 45	2 33	..	5
7¼		Winslow	arr.	3	....	....	5 39	....	8 15	9 45	....	....	....	12 30	1 49	2 37	....	5
			dep.	4	..	..	5 41	7 40	8 18	9 47	..	..	..	12 31	1 50	2 38	..	5
9¼	0	Verney Junction ⊕	arr.	5	....	4 53	....	7 44	8 22	9 51	....	....	....	12 35	1 54	2 42	....	5
			dep.	6	4 4	5 3	5 45	7 45	8 25	9 52	..	..	..	12 37	1 55	2 43	..	5
	2¼	Padbury ......(H)		7	§—Swanbourne Sidings; and arr. 3L52 a.m. (detaches coupled engine)	....	....	....	8 30	....	....	....	....	....	....	2 48	....	..
	4¼	Buckingham ⊕	arr.	8		..	T—Arr. 5.34. Stop not advertised.	..	8 35	..	..	C.O.D. Exchange Sidings arr. 11.15 a.m.	..	..	..	2 53	..	..
			dep.	9		....		....	8 39	....	....		Not advertised.	....	....	2 55	....	..
	9	Fulwell & Westbury	..	10		Mail.		..	8 48	..	..			..	..	3 4	..	..
	12	Brackley ⊕	arr.	11				....	8 53	....	....			....	....	3 9	....	..
			dep.	12				..	8 55	..	..			..	..	3 10	..	..
	16	Cockley Brake Jn. ⊕		13		....		....	9* 2	....	9*53			....	....	3*17	....	..
	17½	Farthinghoe		14		..	..	..	9 6	..	9 57		..	..	..	3 21	..	..
	21¼	BANBURY ⊕	arr.	15		....	....	....	9 13	....	10 4	....	....	....	....	3 28	....	..
11¼		Claydon	dep.	16	4N10	..	..	7 49	..	9 56	..	†—No. 2.	..	12 41	1 59	..	..	5
15		Marsh Gibbon & Poundon		17	....	....	....	7 57	....	10 4	....		....	12 49	2 7	....	....	5
17¼		Launton	..	18	N—L.N.E. Jn. and is arrival time.	..	..	8 1	..	10 8	..		..	N	2 11	..	..	5
19½		Bicester	arr.	19		5 21	6 2	8 5	....	10 12	....	....	....	12 56	2 15	....	....	5
			dep.	20		5 25	6 4	8 10	..	10 14	..	11†13	12 0	12 58	2 17	..	..	5
25½		Islip	arr.	21		....	6 14	....	....	....	....	....	....	....	....	....	....	6
			dep.	22		..	6 15	8 20	..	10 24	..	..	..	1 8	2 26	..	..	6
31¼		OXFORD	arr.	23		5 47	6 25	8 30	....	10 34	....	....	12 20	1 18	2 36	....	....	6

H—Worked as a Halt for 5.28 p.m. Bletchley to Banbury.

No. 10—**N**—Calls at Launton on Wednesdays and Saturday dep. 12.53 p.m., and forward one minute later.

AND BLETCHLEY.

	WEEKDAYS.													SUNDAYS.										
15	16	17	18	19	20	21	23	24	25	26	28	29	30	31	32	31	35	36	37	38	39	40		
	B		B		B		B		B		B		B				B				B			
	To Bedford.										To Wolverton.													
	p.m.		p.m.		p.m.		p.m.		SX p.m.		SO p.m.		a.m.				p.m.				p.m.			
	5 20		7 0						10 30		10 30		10 36				4 45				10 0			
			7 10								10 40		10 46				4 55							
	5 30		7 11								10 41		10 47				4 56							
	5 39		7 21		Mail.				10 49		10 51		10 57				5 6				10 30			
	5 41		7 23						10 54		10 54		11 0				5 8							
	5 46		7 28						10 59		10 59		11 5				5 13							
	5 51		7 33										11 10				5 18							
	5 59		7 41						11 10		11 10		11 18				5 26							
					7 0																		Not advertised.	
					7 8																			
					7*12																			
					7 19																			
			Mail.		7 21																			
					7 27																			
					7 35																			
					7 40		9 25																	
					7 45		9 31																	
	6 3		7 45		7 50				11 14		11 14		11 22				5 30							
	6 4		7 46		7 54		9*36		11 18		11 18		11 26				5 34							
	6 9		7 51		7 59		9 40		11 19		11 19		11 28				5 36							
	6 10		7 53		8 0		9 41		11 24		11 24		11 33				5 41							
	6 15		7 58		8 5		9 46		11 33		11 33		11 42				5 50							
	6 24		8 7		8 14		9 55																	

AND OXFORD.

	WEEKDAYS.												SUNDAYS										
16	17	18	19	20	21	22	23	24	25	26	27	28	31	32	34	35	36	37	38	39	40	41	
B			B			B			B			B					B		B		C		
6.32 p.m. from Blisworth.																					Empty Stock.		
p.m.			p.m.			p.m.			p.m.			a.m.					p.m.		p.m.		p.m.		
			8 15			8 40			10 0			8 46					1 0						
			8 26			8 51			10 12			8 57					1 11						
			8 30			8 55			10 16			9 1					1 15						
			8 31			8 57			10 17			9 2					1 17						
			8 35																				
			8 36			9* 1			10 21			9 6					1 21						
						9 6																	
						9 11																	
									§—Arr. 10.11														
7*14																							
7 18																							
7 25																							
			8 40						10 25			9 10					1 25						
			8 49									9 19					1 30						
			8 53						10 38			9 23					1 38						
			8 57						10 41			9 29					1 43			10 35		11 30	
			8 59									9 38					1 54						
			9 9									9 39					1 55				11 55		
			9 19						10 56			9 49					2 5						

ime-table of Passenger trains from 18th June to 23rd September, 1951.

Mick Morris — British Railways

Chapter Eleven

'Auld Lang Syne'

When Mrs Neville booked a ticket to Bletchley from Banbury in the early 1930's the only other travelling companion on the train for the whole journey was a pig! Now this may be a romantic thought to the lovers of pastoral railways but it was hardly likely to impress the Company. Passenger receipts were never very high on the Banbury branch after 1923; had the line achieved the greater aspirations of Sir Harry Verney and the London and Birmingham Railway it would have been an entirely different story, which must remain nothing more than conjecture. Nevertheless in its unfulfilled role it still gave a good service to the towns and villages that it passed through or near and they in return supported it by a reasonably intensive use of its freight and cattle facilities. Throughout LMS and British Railways ownership the line appears to have been continually suspended in penury, and like many other lines became conditioned to it, knowing that the axe would fall some day, but for the time being it was an easy ambling country railway. It is true to say that the two world wars gave it some sharp jolts, and created new impetus, which was short-lived but by the time of nationalisation the pace was winding very slow indeed. A glance at the time-table for the 1952 period will give some indication of the tenuous condition of the passenger services, and I feel sure that had the line not been selected in 1956 for a single railcar experiment the Buckingham — Banbury section would have ceased to run passenger trains by the mid-fifties.

The experiment was considered at the time as something of a ray of hope for all the many branch lines throughout the United Kingdom that were in a similarly parlous state as the Banbury branch. Hitherto British Railways had run their new diesel multiple units in trains of not less than two vehicles, an exception for this experiment being that the two cars would run independently and be driven from both ends, in the manner of a tram car. The intention was that they would operate the services between Buckingham and Banbury, connecting at Buckingham with a steam push-pull working to Bletchley.

Farthinghoe which had closed when the Blisworth service ceased was not re-opened but two new Halts were opened at Water Stratford and Radclive crossing, between Fulwell and Westbury and Buckingham. Ironically there had been talk of building a station at Water Stratford as early as 1861 which made this a rather belated acquisition for the village. The halts were all timber construction with old wooden sleepers for the surface and unlike all other platforms on the branch were built to the standard height. A simple painted wooden nameboard and some old LNWR oil lamps were all the furnishing they possessed. It was the

Rudimentary platform and L.N.W.R. oil lamps on the new halt at Radclive Crossing, looking towards Banbury.

Len's of Sutton

Water Stratford Halt looking toward Buckingham. Note the concrete sleepers by 'Dow Mac', an early use of these on the branch was in 1946. They were first used by Dow-Mac in 1942.

Len's of Sutton

A scene of great irritation to many passengers and railwaymen for that matter, the change over at Buckingham. The railcar is to form the 4.22

●
Bid to save a branch

IN the hope of averting withdrawal of the branch passenger service, which at present involves a loss of £14,000 a year, two experimental single-unit diesel railcars were brought into use from August 13 on the 16¾ miles section of the L.M.R. Buckingham and Banbury (Merton Street) branch. The cars are similar to those in B.R. multiple-unit diesel trains, but are capable of being driven from either end. Hitherto, of course, the B.R. diesel trains have been run as a minimum two-car formation, and the Buckingham–Banbury scheme is being undertaken as an experiment in the running of single railcars on sections where passenger traffic is very light. The service will be worked by two single-unit cars, one with a seating capacity of 61, the other of 52 second-class passengers. The two intermediate stations (Fulwell & Westbury and Brackley Town) between Banbury and Buckingham will be kept open, and in addition two halts of very simple construction will be built at Radclive and Water Stratford with the object of serving nearby villages. Tickets will be issued by the guard at the halts. The service between Banbury and Buckingham runs in connection with the Buckingham–Bletchley steam service.

●

duty of the Brackley Stationmaster to light the lamps, which must have given a rather poetic glow through the countryside at dusk. As the halts were only one car in length, on the occasions when two cars were running it was necessary to draw forward. There were some suggestion that a third halt should be opened near Buckingham, in the vicinity of the goods yard, but this was never installed. On meeting people who used the service I soon discovered that to say it was well-liked is something of an understatement, the public was fascinated by the railcars, finding them convenient for prams and parcels etc. An edition of *The Times*, made references to, "these little olive green railcars gliding along pleasant countryside", and "Our lighthearted little craft scuttling to and fro". One obvious irritation for a through traveller was the change of trains at Buckingham, and this situation did receive substantial criticism. R.S. Hampson, the Buckingham Stationmaster wrote, "If it appeared romantic, it was certainly inconvenient to many passengers. Every parcel and passenger going beyond Buckingham had to change trains at the station. The meeting of trains and an occasional exchange of horseboxes was like a ritual dance as trains arrived, reversed, changed platforms and departed whence they came". Eighteen months after the start of the experiment this tiresome delay was removed and the cars ran straight through to Bletchley.

A last look at the old and rather derelict looking station front before rejuvenation.
Photomatic — R. Carpenter

1956 and a facelift for the sad looking frontage; the name is simply painted on after the removal of the block lettering of the L.M.S. which replaced that of the L.N.W.R. Changes at nationalisation brcught Banbury (Merton Street) under the control of the ex-G.W.R. Stationmaster. Later in the 1962 boundary movements the entire railway complex at Banbury came under the authority of the London Midland Region.

On the 13th August, 1956 the new service began, and the Banbury station, which had been repainted and generally facelifted for its new and interesting role was prepared to receive the two shining green rail-cars as they arrived from Bletchley, where they had been stored. Alas the evidence of the Banbury station's declining years could not be so easily concealed as the boarding of the roof had reached such a condition as to be a danger to the travellers waiting beneath it. In the previous year most of it had been removed leaving all the bare-ribbed piping and supports apologetically covered in white paint.

When the two cars did arrive it could probably have not been too soon for the waiting officials and newspaper reporter as No.'s M 79901 and M 79900 came speeding through the dismal morning, the reporter des-cribed the scene. "The first train left Merton Street at 7.8 this morning, the weather was wet, rain poured in through the open girder work where once there had been a station roof, soaking the bare planking upon which we stood." The first car would leave singly leaving the other car to form the following train. The seating capacity of each car was 61 and 52 respectively. But it soon became necessary on Banbury market days, Thursday, and for the multitude of shoppers on Saturday to run the cars in tandem on both those days, sometimes with one hundred and twenty in each! The fare to Buckingham was 3s. 9d. (19p) cheap day return, with a half-hour service frequency. As I have already mentioned these speedy and efficient lightweights, built at Derby, soon became popular as they plied back and forth, passing the derelict ghost of Farthinghoe. Shoppers found that taking their prams with them was easily accomplished in the spacious luggage compartment, it was the same for anyone planning to cycle the rest of their way to work, nor need one be inhibited from purchasing any large parcel. Students were able to take up courses at Banbury and travel in from Buckingham and Brackley, with very little waiting around in the chilly months. In a period when British Railways had been regarded by many to be wearing the sombre garb of Executioners there was a mood of optimism for the newly opened service, and that it would almost certainly bring a revival to branch line travel.

On talking to Arthur Grigg about the experiment he praised the machines for consistently good running but did mention one fault that was familiar to both cars, this was a tendency for the brake pistons to stick. An example of such an incident he related to me was when one of the vehicles began to increase speed on the down grade toward Banbury, realising that this speed was now excessive the driver naturally began applying the brakes. Much to his concern and mounting alarm there was no welcoming bite on the wheels to check their flight, no reverberation from the steel panelling as it absorbed the deceleration, only the free and uninterrupted movement of the car as it continued whistling down the hill and the approaching curve that could have been formid-able, had there been any greater train weight involved. The guard soon

First Saturday of operation for railcar No. 79901 as it waits at Banbury to take the 3.45 to Buckingham. Some keen interest appears to have been aroused by the arrival of the novel machine judging by the number of bystanders.

W.A. Camwell

Prams await loading into the spacious luggage compartment of the railcar. Behind the two ladies appear to be a set of recently constructed steps.

Graham Wiltor

Railcar No. 79901 at Radclive Halt on 18th of August 1956 en route for Buckingham.

W.A. Camwell

Buckingham — Banbury railcar appears to have some business at Water Stratford on the 18th of August 1956. New rails for old in the youthful looking concrete sleepers.

W.A. Camwell

Busy days at Buckingham once more. The railcar arrives from Banbury, whence it will return, after running around the loop to the 'down' side.

realised what was happening in the driving cab and told all his passengers to crouch down behind the seats, continuing up to the front where he began to apply all of his physical strength to bring on the hand brake. One can imagine the tense and courageous railwaymen as they speeded across Butcher's Crossing, acutely aware of their responsibility for the passengers crouched in the saloon behind. By the time that they had reached the throat of the station the hand brake was beginning to take effect and the car was dropping below forty miles an hour, fast enough though to alarm the signalman. Luckily for all concerned the action taken was just enough and the car came to rest a matter of inches away from the buffers. The exhausted guard threw himself down on the passenger seat, the driver rested his head in his hands and the passengers rose, recomposed themselves and left without saying a word.

It is quite possible that the fault was soon found and rectified as there is no record of any mishap during their short but intensive service.

In 1959 when the service was not quite three years old talk of closure was in the air once again. British Railways agreed that the cars were well patronised at peak times but claimed that this could not offset the fact that they ran almost empty at normal times. Most of the argument for keeping the service tended to be delivered from the areas of Buckingham, Fulwell and Westbury and Brackley with Banbury seeming largely indifferent; some people in Banbury thought that the line had already closed.

Time-table during railcar period 1958/59.

BANBURY — BLETCHLEY

BRITISH RAILWAYS (L.M.R.) TABLE **6**

WEEKDAYS ONLY

	a.m.	a.m.	a.m.	a.m.	p.m.	p.m.	p.m.	SX a.m.	SO p.m.	p.m.	p.m.	SX p.m.	SO p.m.	SO p.m.	SO p.m.
Banbury (Merton St.)	6 48	9 14	......	11 5	1 45	......	3 45	...	......	5 45	......	7 22	7 22	9 48	10 52
Brackley	7 3	9 30	......	11 20	2 0	......	4 0	...	......	6 0	......	7 37	7 37	10 2	11 7
Fulwell and Westburn	7 8	9 35	......	11 25	2 5	......	4 5	...	......	6 5	...	7 43	7 43	10 8	11 12
Water Stratford Halt	7 12	9 39	......	11 29	2 9	......	4 9	...	......	6 9	...	7 46	7 46	10 11	11 16
Radclive Halt	7 16	9 43	......	11 33	2 13	......	4 13	...	......	6 13	...	7 50	7 50	10 15	11 20
Buckingham { a	7 19	9 46	......	11 36	2 16	......	4 16	...	......	6 16	...	7 54	7 54	10 19	11 23
{ d	7 20	......	9 55	11 37	......	2 35	......	4 36	4 36	......	6 36	7 55	7 55	......	11 24
Padbury	7 24	......	9 59	11 41	......	2 39	......	4 40	4 40	......	6 40	8 0	8 0	......	11 28
Verney Junction { a	7 29	......	......	11 46	......	......	......	......	......	......	6 46	8 4	8 4	......	11 34
{ d	7 30	......	10 4	11 47	......	2 44	......	4 45	4 45	......	6 47	8 5	8 5	......	11 35
Winslow	7 34	......	10 10	11 51	......	2 50	......	4 51	4 51	......	6 52	8 9	8 9	......	11 40
Swanbourne	7 38	......	10 15	11 55	......	2 55	......	4 56	4 56	......	6 57	8 14	8 14	......	11 44
Bletchley	7 47	......	10 25	12 4	......	3 5	......	5 6	5 6	......	7 7	8 23	8 23	......	11 53
Cambridge a	11 31	......	......	1 48	......	5 25	......	......	8 15	......	......	9 57	9 59	......	......
Northampton Cas. a	8 D25	......	......	1 23	......	4 K43	......	6 8	7 31	......	8 29	12 9	12 25	......	1 26

	a.m.	SO a.m.	SX a.m.	a.m.	a.m.	a.m.	SX a.m.	SO a.m.	SO p.m.	SX a.m.	p.m.	p.m.	p.m.	SO p.m.	SO p.m.
Northampton Cas. d	4 21	6 35	6 50	8 0	......	10 0	......	......	12 49	......	2 43	......	4 15	7 52	......
Cambridge d	......	......	......	......	......	9 23	9 38	11 26	11 26	......	......	2 5	6 18	......	......
Bletchley	5 18	7 55	7 55	9 10	......	......	12 30	12 30	1 55	1 55	3 35	......	5 28	8 31	8 50	......
Swanbourne	......	8 4	8 4	9 20	......	......	12 39	12 39	2 5	2 5	3 45	......	5 38	8 45	......
Winslow	......	8 8	8 8	9 25	......	......	12 43	12 43	2 10	2 10	3 50	......	5 44	8 50	......
Verney Junction { a	......	8 12	8 12	9 30	......	......	12 47	12 47	2 15	2 15	3 55	......	5 49	8 55	9 3	......
{ d	......	8 13	8 13	9 31	......	......	12 48	12 48	2 16	2 16	3 56	......	5 50	......	9 4	......
Padbury	......	8 17	8 17	9 35	......	......	12 52	12 52	2 20	2 20	4 0	......	5 54	......	9 8	......
Buckingham { a	5 38	8 22	8 22	9 41	......	......	12 56	12 56	2 26	2 26	4 6	......	6 0	......	9 13	......
{ d	5 47	8 25	8 25	......	9 52	......	12 57	12 57	2 30	2 30	......	4 30	6 30	......	9 14	10 23
Radclive Halt	......	8 27	8 27	......	9 54	......	12 59	12 59	2 32	2 32	......	4 32	6 32	......	9 16	......
Water Stratford Halt	5 B51	8 31	8 31	......	9 58	1 3	1 3	2 36	2 36	......	4 36	6 36	......	9 20	......
Fulwell and Westbury	5 54	8 35	8 35	......	10 2	1 7	1 7	2 40	2 40	......	4 40	6 40	......	9 24	......
Brackley	6 4	8 41	8 41	......	10 8	1 13	1 13	2 46	2 46	......	4 46	6 46	......	9 29	......
Banbury (Merton St.)	6 19	8 56	8 56	......	10 23	1 28	1 28	3 1	3 1	......	5 17	7 1	......	9 44	10 48

B—Monday only. D—8 52 on Sat. K—4 25 on Sat. SO or S—Saturday only. SX—Not Saturday.

153

On the 5th December, 1959 the line was visited by R.C. Riley, a name that is familiar to all who have a keen interest in railways; an example of his accomplished skill with a camera is included in this history. An additional fascination is a superbly detailed account written by Mr Riley, of a journey from Bletchley to Banbury in an ordinary 2-car DMU set on the 12.30 pm from Bletchley, it appears that M 79900 on arrival at Bletchley retired to the carriage sheds. The description of the journey is highly poignant and although only seventeen years ago it is just as much a part of history as the day the line opened.

"Verney Junction — Part of the Quainton Road branch survives for a short distance, and is used, with the siding space, to house condemned coaches and new covered goods wagon frames. A separate platform exists for the former branch, so that trains for Oxford or Buckingham use an island platform. The Banbury branch curves away to right, driver collects staff from signalman (to do this he must cross cab and operate deadman's button — 7 seconds delay allowed). Line becomes single at once and for the whole of its length continues through pleasant farmland.

2¼ miles Padbury — Small station, single platform, brick building. Small pair of steps on platform for boarding train. Cluster of houses near station. One passenger joined here. Line climbs on and crosses river deep cutting on approach to 4½ miles, Buckingham — Double line crossing station. About twenty-five passengers joined here, and a few alighted. Porter brought staff to driver. Brick buildings on both platforms. Small coal siding behind right-hand platform. Station near the town, and good view of fine parish church. Goods yard about half a mile beyond station beside milepost five. Gradient easier, though still adverse. 5¾ miles Radclive Halt — small platform lit by three oil lamps, one passenger joined to whom the guard issued a ticket. Line climbs more sharply.

8½ miles Water Stratford Halt — Small platform, ten passengers joined here. Platform right beside village. Line still climbing. Beyond here small road level-crossing manned by crossing keeper, after which gradient eases.

9 miles Fulwell and Westbury — Wooden building. About twenty passengers joined train. Level crossing beyond station, also very small signal box with signals to protect the crossing. Line climbs again. By this time the two car set was becoming quite full. Single line passes under the Great Central main line, which curves and later can be seen in the distance as it approaches Brackley.

12 miles Brackley Town — Crossing station, brick buildings both sides. Stationmaster here. Several passengers alighted and about thirty joined. Staff exchanged. Goods yard before station. Gradient eases beyond here, although short climb after road over-bridge, then eases again. By this time first class compartment full, to prevent overcrowding in second class — in any case train second class only. All appear to be

The South Bedfordshire Locomotive Club branch line tour 'The Banburian' arrives at Farthinghoe behind ex-LNWR 7F 0-8-0 No. 48930 on Saturday, 22nd September, 1962. The single siding at the left of the running line is well overgrown whilst the latter is remarkably neat and clean.

David Mills

bonafide travellers too and only one other railway enthusiast identifiable. Further on right hand side original formation of the old SMJ (N&B) line curves in at Cockley Brake Junction, the signal box of which has long since disappeared. Gradient falls slightly beyond here, and train reached a speed of about 55 mph. Soon after in the heart of the country miles from anywhere the closed station of Farthinghoe is passed, a still intact wooden building. Line curves round and runs for last half mile or so nearly parallel to the original Great Western Railway's line from Oxford to Banbury before entering 21¾ miles Banbury (Merton Street). Signal box about a hundred yards beyond platform. Driver exhibited staff to signalman but did not surrender it. Considerable number of cattle wagons in sidings — Banbury cattle market very large and important, hence heavy rail traffic so line will not be closed to freight traffic. Banbury has single island platform, very low, and one pair of steps provided. Passenger trains use only eastern face of platform. Only struts of all-over roof survive, long since devoid of glazing. Platform and side of walls of wooden construction and gas lit. In fact there were 104 passengers on this train, the 1.26 arrival, and over 50 on the 3.9 pm. Strengthening of train to two coaches mainly intended for return train at 5.50 pm which is normally heavily loaded. Closure warning notices exhibited, but date not shown. Originally intended for 2.1.60 but understood to be deferred for two weeks owing to failure to come to agreement with Bus Company to re-substitute services. Bus Company said to require subsidy before operating unremunerative service.''

Table 59

OXFORD AND BLETCHLEY

WEEKDAYS ONLY

Miles	Miles									SX	SO					SX	SO				
			a.m.	a.m.	a.m.			a.m.	a.m.	a.m.	a.m.	a.m.	a.m.	a.m.			a.m.	a.m.		a.m.	a.m.
0	—	OXFORD ... dep	...	...	6 24	...	...	...	...				...	...	7 57	...		9 44	
5¾	—	Islip			6 37										8 10			9 57	
11¼	—	Bicester London Road			6 46										8 19			10 6	
14	—	Launton			6 50										8 23			
16½	—	Marsh Gibbon & Poundon			6 54										8 26			
20	—	Claydon			7 2										8 33			
—	0	BUCKINGHAM ... dep						7 14		7 45	8 25									11
—	2¼	Padbury						7 17		7 49	8 28									11
21¾	4½	Verney Junction ... dep			7 6			7 22		7 54	8 33	8 38								11
24	—	Winslow			7 11			7 27		7 59		8 43								11
25¾	—	Swanbourne			7 15			7 31		8 4	8 40	8 47								11
31¼	—	BLETCHLEY { arr			7 25			7 40		8D13	8 49	9 4						10 35		11
		{ dep	6 35	7 14	...			8 5	8 10			9 6	9 25	9 25			10 38	11 20	

			SO			SO	SO			SO	SX	Th SO		SX	SO			
			p.m.	a.m.	p.m.	p.m.	p.m.	p.m.	p.m.	p.m.	p.m.	p.m.		p.m.	p.m.		p.m.	p.m.
OXFORD ... dep			11 27			1 10								2 48	2 55			
Islip			11 41			1 21								3 1	3 8			
Bicester London Road			11 50			1 30								3 10	3 17			
Launton			11 54											3 14	3 21			
Marsh Gibbon & Poundon			11 58											3 18	3 25			
Claydon			12 5											3 25	3 32			
BUCKINGHAM ... dep						1 37					2 45						4 35	
Padbury						1 40					2 48						4 38	
Verney Junction ... dep			12 9			1 45					2 53		3 29	3 36			4 43	
Winslow			12 14			1 50					2 58		3 34	3 41			4 48	
Swanbourne			12 18			1 54					3 2		3 38	3 45			4 52	
BLETCHLEY { arr			12 28			2 3					3 11		3 48	4 0			5G 1	
{ dep	12 7		1 10	1 42		2 0			2 50	3 10			3 53	4 2		4 22		

			SX	SX				SO	SX					SO	SX	SX
			p.m.	p.m.		p.m.	p.m.	p.m.	p.m.		p.m.	p.m.	p.m.	p.m.	p.m.	p.m.
OXFORD ... dep						5 18					6 48		7 55			10 5
Islip						5 31					7 1					11
Bicester London Road						5 41					7 11		8 15			11
Launton						5 45					7 15					11
Marsh Gibbon & Poundon						5 49					7 19					11
Claydon						5 56					7 26					11 2
BUCKINGHAM ... dep						5 57							7 45			
Padbury						6 0							7 48			
Verney Junction ... dep						6 0	6 6				7 30		7 53			11
Winslow						6 5	6 11				7 35		7 58			11
Swanbourne						6 9	6 15				7 39		8 2			11
BLETCHLEY { arr						6 19	6 24				7 48		8 11	8 37		11
{ dep	5 38	6 15						6 46	6 46		7 54				8 47	8 49

The Bletchley — Buckingham service published in the time-table of 1964 and consequently the last publication of passenger trains on the Banbury branch.

Mick Morris — British Railways

156

BLETCHLEY AND OXFORD
WEEKDAYS ONLY

		🄱 a.m.	a.m.	🄱 a.m.	a.m.	a.m.	🄱 a.m.	a.m.	a.m.	SX a.m.	SO a.m.	🄱 SX a.m.
BLETCHLEY	dep	5 30	6 35	7 10	7 38		7 55		9 25		10 52	
Swanbourne				7 20	7 48		8 4		9 35		11 2	
Winslow		5 45		7 24	7 52		8 8		9 39		11 6	
Verney Junction	dep			7 28	7 56		8 12		9 43		11 10	
Padbury				7 32			8 16				11 14	
BUCKINGHAM	arr		6 57	7 38			8 21				11 19	
Claydon	dep				8 0				9 47			
Marsh Gibbon & Poundon					8 6				9 53			
Launton					8 10				9 57			
Bicester London Road		6 6			8 16				10 3			
Islip		6 15			8 25				10 12			
OXFORD	arr	6 27			8 37				10 24			

		a.m.											SX	SX
BLETCHLEY	dep	11 52	1 5		1 48	2 10		3 50	4 0			5 7	5 22
Swanbourne			1 14		1 58	2 19		4 0	4 9			5 16	5 31
Winslow		12 4	1 18		2 2	2 23		4 4	4 13			5 20	5 35
Verney Junction	dep		1 22		2 6	2 27		4 8	4 17			5 24	5 39
Padbury			1 26			2 31			4 21				5 43
BUCKINGHAM	arr		1 31			2 36			4 26				5 48
Claydon	dep				2 10			4 12				5 27	
Marsh Gibbon & Poundon					2 16			4 18				5 33	
Launton					2 20			4 22				5 37	
Bicester London Road		12 22		1 55	2 25		4E32				5 41	
Islip				2 4	2 34		4 41				5 50	
OXFORD	arr	12 42		2 15	2 46		4 53				6 4	

									SX	SO	SX	SX
BLETCHLEY	dep	6 46		8 13	8 55	9 15	10 22	10 22				
Swanbourne		6 55			9 5	9 25	10 32	10 32				
Winslow		6 59			9 9	9 29	10 36	10 36				
Verney Junction	dep	7 3			9 13	9 33						
Padbury		7 7										
BUCKINGHAM	arr	7 12										
Claydon	dep				9 17	9 37	10 42	10 42				
Marsh Gibbon & Poundon					9 43	9 47						
Launton						9 47						
Bicester London Road				8 36	9 28	9 53	10 53	10 53				
Islip				8 45	9 37	10 2						
OXFORD	arr			8 58	9 51	10 14	11 13	11 13				

🄱—Second Class only.
A—Arrives Blunham 11.10 a.m.
B—Arrives Willington 7.32 p.m.
C—Arrives Sandy 6.11 p.m.
D—On Saturdays arrives Bletchley 8.16 a.m.
E—Arrives Bicester London Road 4.27 p.m.
F—On Fridays depart Kempston Hardwick 3.42 p.m. arrive Bedford
    St. John's 3.48 p.m.
G—On Saturdays arrives Bletchley 5.3 p.m.
H—Arrives Blunham 2.48 p.m.
ThSO—Thursdays and Saturdays only.
SO—Saturdays only.
SX—Saturdays excepted.

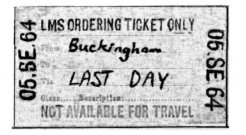

Taken during the railcar service, the grassy platform cannot be any great encouragement to the travellers. The lady on the furthest seat appears to be looking at the 'bare-ribbed' station roof with dismay.

Len's of Sutton

Banbury station on 26th November, 1960. The end is only one month away for the passenger service and this cheerless winter day only serves to emphasise the melancholy future. Note the L.N.W.R. seats and wooden 'stop block' at platform end.

R.C. Riley

Dick returned to the line and repeated his journey in the November of the following year where he found the situation to be much the same as he had left it on his previous visit.

Saturday 26th November, 1960. "Diesel Car M 79900 arrived at Bletchley 1.26, departed for Buckingham 1.55. The station staff and train crew said nothing official had been told to them with regard to the supposed closure of the line to passengers supposed to take place in January 1961, no notices were posted concerning the closure. The clerk said that up to last week the Midland Red Omnibus Co. still had not agreed to provide a substitute bus service, but a further meeting took place at end of week. From the down train there were 78 passengers with 5 prams alighted, while 13 passengers and 2 prams left on the up train; also a trolley load of parcels unloaded and loaded respectively. This said the clerk, presented a misleading picture and often trains ran on weekdays with no passengers at all."

The hard financial facts behind the experiment were published in the following year by the Central Transport Consultative Committee (CTCC) and printed in the "Trains Illustrated" in July 1960.

"The CTCC does perform one service in publishing the fullest financial details of the Banbury — Buckingham railcar experiment we have seen. Before the service was dieselised, the steam push and pull workings had been losing £14,000 per annum and receipts were averaging no more than £50 per month. The railcars boosted receipts to £250 — £300 a month and reduced operating costs by about £300 a month, the exact amount depending on the season. Nevertheless, even the best month's working of the whole three-year experiment still showed a deficit of £400 and the annual loss could not be improved beyond a figure of £4,700."

Finally the day was officially decreed when the last passenger train would run from Banbury to Buckingham, an added poignancy in the fact that it was to be the last day of 1960.

During the final day's running there had been full trains of railway enthusiasts with cameras and notebooks taking advantage of the last opportunity to ride over these metals, but by the evening and the very last train the station at Banbury had become far less populated as only a handful of people stood on the platform, two reporters, the driver of the railcar, Fred Sear, two other railway staff and a sprinkling of passengers. Faint across the town some early New Year's Eve revellers sang out a rather premature 'Auld Lang Syne' that was appropriate to the dimly lit station, as if their chorus was assigned by fates of which they themselves were unaware. One of the reporters was Graham Wilton from the Banbury Advertiser who had booked to ride the last train and wrote an invaluable description of these last few minutes.

" . . . the bare-ribbed station appearing now like a stranded whale. The waiting room was thick with dust and the old iron stove had not been lit, there was dirt and litter everywhere making the new diesel appear like an intruder amid the decay and decomposition, hardly a prepossessing sight for the would be traveller."

Not a prepossessing sight but possible a more convenient one as the final bargain with the Midland Red Bus Company was drastic in the extreme, to replace what had virtually been a half-hour service with what amounted to two buses a day, one at 7.25 am and another at 3.31 pm. Local people complained at the meagre substitute but they were too few, and in what became a familiar pattern of protest and argument the weight of official policy gradually settled, like a tombstone.

At Brackley Arthur Marriott had already found employment elsewhere, not on the railway. The Stationmaster Mr Ernest Clare was to become Chief Booking Clerk at Leighton Buzzard whilst Sid Green Signalman/Porter who was replaced at Fulwell and Westbury by 'Dolly' Chapman and had spent many years service on the branch where he would remain for the time being, spoke to Graham Wilton about the end of Brackley as a passenger station. He referred to the fact that the line would be kept open for the one iron ore train from Cropredy to the smelting works at Wellingborough, plus the cattle trains, and for this service the staff would have to be maintained almost to the same extent as when the railcars were in service. Concerning the railcars Sid claimed that the Banbury — Buckingham section showed a far more prosperous return than the more expensive Buckingham — Bletchley section, a view that was substantiated from many other sources.

Brackley on 12th August, 1961. The wagon turntable in the foreground has survived well, so too have the timber buffer stops along that road. Interesting similarity with the platform fencing and that of Farthinghoe.

Just after passenger closure; the fresh looking notice on the notice board is to that effect.

Len's of Sutton

The presence of ore wagons on the running side of the platform indicates that this photograph was probably taken not long after the railcars ceased.

Len's of Sutton

One interesting footnote to the closure at Brackley was a brave but unsuccessful attempt by the Brackley Borough Council to buy or rent their station and line as far as Buckingham, but the clouds were gathering for Buckingham as well.

Goods traffic continued to run through to Banbury with Standard class '3's and '4's but when one of these ran down a siding then suddenly lurched over at a crazy angle, pushing the chairs through the rotting sleepers, then had to be hurriedly propped with long poles, things were getting so bad as to be dangerous. Further to this the iron ore trains began to be routed over the ex-SMJ north from Banbury. Added to this was the fact that British Railways had not made any special provision for new cattle carrying vehicles in their modernisation programme and were no longer encouraging this form of traffic, and the last strands that held Banbury (Merton Street) were severed. The Buckingham — Banbury section was finally closed to all traffic in December 1964.

The two halts of Radclive and Water Stratford were removed and the derelict Fulwell and Westbury became slowly vandalised. The railcars started a new service between Bletchley and Buckingham as soon as the former section closed, this continued to appear on the timetable until 1964, when that too came under review for closure. Early in that year the villagers of Padbury were most indignant and voiced their protests with newspaper announcements, posters and meetings, they loathed to lose their railway without a fight. But with monotonous inevitability the last day and the last train arrived when the people of Buckingham and Padbury were forced to relinquish an old friend in the only railway they had ever known. Mrs Allen punched her very last ticket and gave it to one of her sons who waved goodbye from the crowded train as it ran over exploding detonators and wailed 'Auld Lang Syne' down the station. At Buckingham the staff had already said their goodbyes, Stationmaster R.S. Hampson, Signalman Harold Plant and Signalman/ Porter Ron Brookes; after 100 years of service, it was not easy to comprehend that it was all over.

During February 1967 track lifting was in full vigour, at the rapid rate of 600 yards a day. The line was now worked as an engineers siding with the lifting gang in complete control. The speed limit of fifteen miles an hour was borne out by necessity as any attempt to exceed up to twenty miles an hour proved the abominable condition of the track. The site of Cockley Brake Junction was reached by mid-March. A type 2 of Bletchley shed propelled a rake of empties to the site each morning, where Messrs Eagres' crane loaded sleepers and rails into the wagons, rails being cut to a more manageable length of about four feet. Later in the same month some difficulties were experienced in a cutting and the sleepers were loaded into lorries which took them to the loading dock at Brackley ex. LNWR, to be loaded onto the lifting train at that point. Intense bustle ensued at the Brackley yard with D7502 supplying the locomotive traction and a shuttle of lorries creaking like tumbrils with their heavy loads. A marked contrast to the now silent and dismal spectacle of Banbury (Merton St.).

One interesting development that took place a year before the previous scene, on February 16th, 1966, was the movement of an 0-6-0 diesel shunter from the depot of R. Fenwick & Co., Brackley to the Central Electricity Board works at Hams Hill. R. Fenwick & Co. specialised in the purchase, hire and sales of second hand locomotives, from their depot adjacent to the goods yard at Brackley. Various diesel locomotives were held in stock, also a tiny Peckett named *Mesozoic* and a Longmoor Military Railway open-sided railcar 9110. The locomotive despatched on the 16th of February was a 350 hp shunter, A.W. & Co. D58 of 1935, formerly LMS 7063. Added to LMS stock P. 13/36, loaned to the Government P. 9/40 and taken out of LMS stock owners in 1958. Special arrangements were made with British Rail to run the ex-War Department engine down the branch on a Wednesday holding it at Buckingham for a further twenty four hours until it could be routed through the schedules on its mainline run through Bletchley to Coalville. In charge of the temporary signalling arrangements was relief signalman Sid Sellers who had operated the Brackley Box thirty-five years previously. This occasion appears to be the very last time that any locomotive preceded the track lifting loco along the metals of the branch.

Banbury cattle pens in 1975 with the Midland Marts complex on the left. Between the pens and beneath British Road Services wire fence are the sloping setts installed by the railway for easy drainage. The rails are still in the ground, one side being used as a 'stop' for the rear wheels of the lorries.

Brian Garland

THE BUCKINGHAMSHIRE RAILWAY

by Charles Whitehall of Gawcott.

The first sod of the Buckinghamshire Railway was turned by Mr Field of
Rugby, the Company's head Physician.

Now to describe the great Bucks line,
   I think I'll have a try,
And tell you how the work went on,
   Through hills both hard and high.

The embankments stout, and Viaducts,
   The valleys for to cross;
The numerous yards of earth brought there,
   Removed by man and horse.

Then the contractors soon appeared,
   Each man his ground to take;
The trees were felled, the hedges grubbed,
   Way for the rails to make.

John Tomkin did the first peg drive,
   When they did first survey,
And he is working for the company now,
   Unto this very day!

But within four miles of Buckingham Town,
   The work has difficult been;
The hills were thick, the valleys deep,
   Crossing the river between.

At the entrance of the county,
   On Oxfordshire's north side,
We first encountered Bacon Hill,
   A cutting deep and wide.

'Twas Bacon's Wood a place of note,
   A favourite game reserve,
But the game was killed, the wood felled,
   The company for to serve.

The rocks were hard, so hard and strong,
   All human strength defied;
Much blasting powder they did use
   The stone for to divide.

The largest arch, near Buckingham
  And on the stoutest plan,
Is cross the stream near Tingewick Mill,
  'Tis fifty full feet span.

Both faced and capped with Derby stone,
  Which is both strong and rare;
And a vast expense it must have been
  To bring it from Derbyshire.

And next, a stout brick arch you'll find,
  Full span across the rail;
It's on the Banbury turnpike road,
  And looks o'er Buckingham Vale.

And next, a three arch viaduct
  Was built across Bath Lane;
But, owing to wet, the crowns fell in,
  And so it still remains.

And next, we find a girder bridge,
  To cross the Padbury Road,
Not very high, but stout and strong,
  To bear the ponderous load.

This is a girder bridge,
  And very great the length,
It is more than thirty feet,
  And of tremendous strength.

This bridge is a 'skew' girder called,
  Is sixty eight feet long,
And here three girders are put on
  To make it stout and strong:

This bridge does cross the Claydon Road,
  While known as the 'Ox lanes',
The girders cast at Leamington,
  By Messrs. Smith and James.

And to all concerned upon the line,
  Who moved the clay and rocks,
I am your humble servant still,
  Charles Whitehall, Gawcott, Bucks.

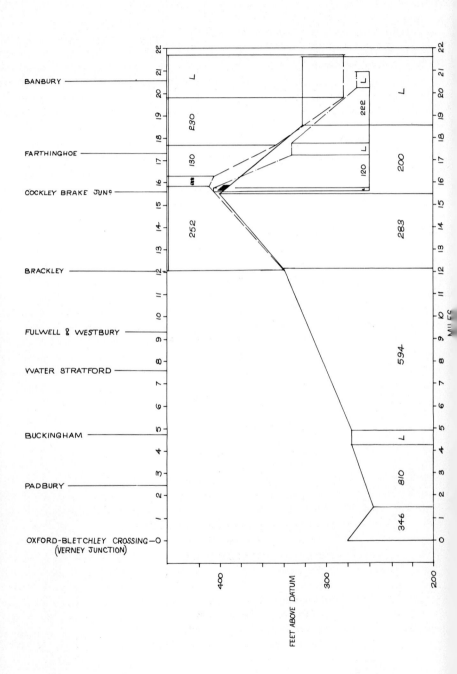

BANBURY

FARTHINGHOE

COCKLEY BRAKE JUNᶜ

BRACKLEY

FULWELL & WESTBURY

WATER STRATFORD

BUCKINGHAM

PADBURY

OXFORD-BLETCHLEY CROSSING—0
(VERNEY JUNCTION)

FEET ABOVE DATUM

MILES

GRADIENT PROFILE

Research has not yet uncovered a full gradient profile of the line as built. The diagram therefore shows three superimposed profiles, two being taken from engineers' surveys.

1. (Continuous line.) From the 1845 survey for the whole line (Tring to Banbury) starting from the crossing point on the Bletchley — Oxford line. The heights are above the datum '396 feet below the top of the rails on the London & Birmingham Railway under bridge 75, near 31¼ miles from London.'

   Note that this proposal includes a 510 yard tunnel at Cockley Brake.

2. (Broken line.) From the 1846 survey for the Banbury extension from Brackley.

   The datum for this is given as 'passing the cemetery at Brackley the top of the rails are 331 ft. 34 ins. (yes 34 ins.) below the upper surface of the stone sill of the doorway of the chapel in the burial ground called the Lower End Burial Ground.'

   Since there is no way of relating this to the datum in (1) above this profile is shown as starting at Brackley on the 1845 survey. Viewing the level land at the site of the cemetery it is also difficult to understand the dimension 331 ft. 34 ins. on this survey. The extension survey deletes the Cockley Brake tunnel by climbing a further 15 ft. before descending to Banbury. Banbury station is shown 18 ft. below the level indicated in 1845!

3. (Chain dot.) From a gradient profile of the Stratford & Midland Junction line, covering the section Cockley Brake to Banbury.

   The profile has been drawn by taking the position of Cockley Brake on the map of the 1846 survey and starting this profile at that point on the 1 in 252 gradient. A short level before descending to Farthinghoe and Banbury appears to maintain adequate height to avoid constructing a tunnel. The descent to Farthinghoe at 1 in 120 is the steepest on the line, and Banbury is again lower than in the 1845 survey, this time by 25 ft. Since this profile was drawn after the line was built it is assumed to be correct.

   Some inconsistencies may be observed from the photographs, on gradient posts. These could be due to alterations being made any time after the plans here included were submitted to the appropriate county offices — and officially recorded. All trace of any modified survey appears to have vanished from the face of the earth, should any reader be aware of such information extant — the author would be pleased to know, via the publisher.

Skew bridge north of Brackley, shortly before demolition in 1976. The new by-pass road that has rendered it useless is in the foreground.

Brian Garland

Crossing.	Situated between	Whether there are indicators.	Whether there are signals.	Whether gates are interlocked with the signals.	Remarks.
Warkworth	Banbury and Farthinghoe	No	No	No	
Fulwell and Westbury...	Fulwell and Buckingham............	Yes	Yes	Yes	
Bacon's House	,, ,, ...	Yes	No	No	
Radclive....................	,, ,, ...	No	No	No	

List of Level Crossings from Working Appendix. At Warkworth Crossing between Farthinghoe and Banbury, known locally as 'Butcher's Crossing', the gates were not fastened across the rails for access of cattle and pedestrians but opened and closed onto the thoroughfare. Closing by the keeper would be according to times and when the engine had given a customary whistle after slowing down some two hundred yards away.

L.M.S. 1937 — Cyril Gibbins

DUTY OF GATEMEN, CAMBRIDGE, OXFORD, BANBURY, DUNSTABLE, AYLESBURY AND ST. ALBANS BRANCHES.

Level crossing gates on the above branches will be placed across the railway and kept op~~ for road traffic during the periods shown below, the signals during such time being kept at dang~~

Drivers must stop at each level crossing for the fireman to open the gates and the guard~~ close the gates, unless special arrangements have been made otherwise :—

Branch.	Period during which gates are placed across the railway and signals kept at danger.
Cambridge to Bedford ..	After passage of last booked train Saturday and between booked trains Sunday 5.10 a.m. Monday.
Bedford to Bletchley ..	After passage of last up freight Sunday morning and between booked trains Sunday 3.15 a.m. Monday.
Oxford	After passage of last booked train Saturday and between booked trains Sunday to 5.0 a.~~ Monday, except at Claydon and Launton when the gates will be across the railw~ from 6.0 a.m. Sunday. A man will travel between Verney Junction and Launt~ with the 6.30 a.m. empty milk, Bletchley to Islip and the 7.50 a.m. milk, Islip Bletchley, and will open and close the level crossing gates and deal with these trai~ at Claydon and Launton.
Banbury	Weeknights, after passage of last booked train (Saturdays excepted) to 7.0 a.m. and la~ booked train on Saturday to 8.0 a.m. Sunday and between booked trains on Sund~ to 7.0 a.m. Monday.

Bridge Two from Verney Junction, the girdered section on the right is where the lines were removed. The bracing on the left is the space of the unrealised down line.

Brian Garland

Price £2.95 net

This book traces the history of the railway that once ran
from Verney Junction to Banbury. The contents include
many interesting photographs, maps, plans and timetables
together with a detailed and well written description of each
station along the line.

Oxford Publishing Co.   902888 87